Ten Steps Toward Greater Operational Efficiency in Higher Education

Featuring a diverse cohort of seasoned leaders in higher education, this book outlines a flexible, ten-step framework for achieving operational efficiency and building a robust internal infrastructure across any functional area within an institution.

The framework identifies ten essential components for creating an effective, student-centered, and equitable functional area: navigating change and context, data, budgeting, strategic planning, day-to-day operations, university policy and procedure, organizational staffing, training and development, communication and collaboration, and strategic enrollment management. Each chapter examines one of these components while providing practical steps for implementation and equipping leaders with the knowledge and tools they need to foster positive change within their roles.

Whether an emerging leader or a senior professional, this text is designed to support all higher education directors, deans, provosts, and division leaders in their administrative goals.

Carlos Gooden is Executive Director at the Marilyn Davies College of Business at the University of Houston-Downtown, Houston, USA.

Mike Hoffshire is Assistant Dean for Admissions and Student Affairs at the Herbert Wertheim School of Optometry and Vision Science at the University of California, Berkeley, USA.

Ten Steps Toward Greater Operational Efficiency in Higher Education

An Administrator Playbook

Edited by Carlos Gooden and Mike Hoffshire

Routledge
Taylor & Francis Group
NEW YORK AND LONDON

Designed cover image: Getty Images

First published 2026
by Routledge
605 Third Avenue, New York, NY 10158

and by Routledge
4 Park Square, Milton Park, Abingdon, Oxon, OX14 4RN

Routledge is an imprint of the Taylor & Francis Group, an informa business

© 2026 selection and editorial matter, Carlos Gooden and Mike Hoffshire; individual chapters, the contributors

The right of Carlos Gooden and Mike Hoffshire to be identified as the authors of the editorial material, and of the authors for their individual chapters, has been asserted in accordance with sections 77 and 78 of the Copyright, Designs and Patents Act 1988.

All rights reserved. No part of this book may be reprinted or reproduced or utilised in any form or by any electronic, mechanical, or other means, now known or hereafter invented, including photocopying and recording, or in any information storage or retrieval system, without permission in writing from the publishers.

For Product Safety Concerns and Information please contact our EU representative GPSR@taylorandfrancis.com. Taylor & Francis Verlag GmbH, Kaufingerstraße 24, 80331 München, Germany.

Trademark notice: Product or corporate names may be trademarks or registered trademarks, and are used only for identification and explanation without intent to infringe.

ISBN: 978-1-032-87671-9 (hbk)
ISBN: 978-1-032-87617-7 (pbk)
ISBN: 978-1-003-53385-6 (ebk)

DOI: 10.4324/9781003533856

Typeset in Palatino
by Newgen Publishing UK

Contents

About the Editors vii
List of Contributors viii
Acknowledgments xv
Introduction xvi
Mike Hoffshire and Carlos Gooden

1 Navigating Context and Change 1
Carlos Gooden and Mike Hoffshire

2 Harnessing and Leveraging Data as a Leader in
Higher Education 13
Erica Ogburn and Jeremy Lane

3 Aligning Resources: Understanding the Budget
Process 27
Emily Erwin

4 Creating and Implementing a Strategic Plan 41
Mike Hoffshire

5 Knowing the Rules to Be Good at the Game:
Understanding University Policy and Procedure 53
Sonia Valencia

6 Leadership in Day-to-Day Operations of Higher
Education Administration 65
Melvin (Jai) Jackson and Kevin McClain

7 Navigating Organizational Structure, Roles, and
Staffing Changes 80
Tracy Pascua Dea

8 Training and Development: The Keys to Building Successful and Sustainable Teams 92
Nicole Caridad Ralston, Kevin Lewis, and Shawn Gaines

9 Leading Through Effective Communication: Strategies for Collaboration 104
Christy Heaton and Nick Fuselier

10 Everyone Recruits, Everyone Retains 118
Christian Alberto

11 Conclusion 133
Carlos Gooden and Mike Hoffshire

Index 141

About the Editors

Carlos Gooden, Ph.D. (he/him), began his career in admissions 15 years ago as a student tour guide at his alma mater. He has since held professional roles in admissions, marketing, and orientation at both the undergraduate and graduate level. Gooden has served at a variety of institutions—including large public universities, private universities, a Catholic university, and a historically Black college and university (HBCU)—bringing a broad and diverse perspective to his work. He earned his Ph.D. in Educational Administration, with research focused on admissions policies and access at urban public institutions. Gooden currently serves as Executive Director at the Marilyn Davies College of Business, University of Houston–Downtown.

Mike Hoffshire, Ph.D. (he/him), is a student affairs and higher education professional, educator, consultant, and speaker with a passion for student success. He serves as the Assistant Dean for Admissions and Student Affairs at the Herbert Wertheim School of Optometry and Vision Science, University of California, Berkeley. Hoffshire's work focuses on best practices in admissions, student retention, and academic success. His professional experience spans multiple functional areas, including academic affairs, admissions, gender and sexuality centers, new student orientation, student success, and residence life. He continues to lead an active research agenda aimed at addressing challenges faced by educational institutions. In addition, he serves as an adjunct faculty member in certificate and master's-level based higher education programs.

Contributors

Christian Alberto, Ed.D. (he/him), is the Director of Admissions & Enrollment Management at the SUNY College of Optometry, where he brings over a decade of experience leading holistic admissions, recruitment, enrollment, and orientation efforts while advancing equity and inclusion. A data-driven scholarly practitioner, he serves on the Institutional Research and Planning Committee and recently led the development of recruitment, branding, and strategic partnerships plan for SUNY Optometry's forthcoming extension campus. Beyond SUNY, he has co-taught an Educational Policy course in the University of Pittsburgh's Ed.D. program, offering practitioner insights on leading effective change in education. Dr. Alberto earned his Ed.D. from Pitt—where his dissertation focused on culturally responsive strategies to expand the racially minoritized student pipeline—along with an M.S. in Higher Education Administration from CUNY and a B.A. in Psychology from the University at Buffalo. A 2022 SUNY Hispanic Leadership Institute Fellow, he is intentional about advancing institutions, empowering teams, and helping students unlock and realize their full potential.

Tracy Pascua Dea, Ph.D. (she/her), is the Academic Climate Program Director at the University of California, Berkeley. She was the former Chief Diversity Officer and Executive Director of Student Services in the School of Journalism. She has more than 20 years of experience in diversity, equity, inclusion, belonging and justice, organizational climate and culture, faculty development, student success, and leadership and systems coaching. Her higher education experience, research, and teaching focus on the lived experiences of first-generation and historically marginalized populations, strengths-based institutional change, and the power of narratives for social change. Her experience as a first- generation student and her families' immigration journey from the Philippines fuels her passion for transformational individual and organizational change. She holds a Ph.D. in Higher Education Administration and B.A. in Psychology from Saint Louis University, and an M.A. in Counseling Psychology from Boston College. She is a certified Organizational Relationship Systems Coach and Gallup-Certified Strengths Coach.

Emily Erwin, Ph.D. (she/her), is Associate Professor of Curricular Analytics in the School of Veterinary Medicine at Louisiana State University (LSU). She most recently served as the Vice Chancellor of Academic Affairs and Institutional Effectiveness for River Parishes Community College in Gonzales, Louisiana. Dr. Erwin brings over 20 years of experience in education, having served in roles related to institutional research, public policy, enrollment management, student services, academic affairs, and institutional effectiveness. She began her career as a high school teacher in the East Baton Rouge Parish Public School System in Louisiana. She then worked at Louisiana State University (LSU), serving in the Office of Budget and Planning and then as Associate Registrar and Institutional Research Analyst at the LSU Law Center. She also served as Senior Policy Analyst for the Louisiana Board of Regents, playing a key role in statewide higher education policy development and analysis. Additionally, she served as the Chief Enrollment Management Officer for the Louisiana Community and Technical College System. Dr. Erwin teaches as an adjunct instructor in the Graduate School of Education at LSU. She holds a B.S. in Secondary Education (History concentration) and an M.P.A. from LSU and obtained her Ph.D. in Higher Education Administration from the University of New Orleans.

Nick Fuselier, Ph.D. (he/him), serves as Assistant Professor in the Department of Leadership, Research, and Foundations at the University of Colorado, Colorado Springs. Prior to his current role as a faculty member, Dr. Fuselier worked as a student affairs professional in a variety of functional areas including first-year experience, college access and student success programs, leadership development, service learning, and community engagement. He was recognized as an Annuit Coeptis Emerging

Professional by ACPA-College Student Educators International in 2017 and served on its Governing Board from 2020 to 2023. A qualitative researcher, his work centers on how colleges and universities can be radically transformed to meet the needs and lived experiences of those most marginalized in campus communities. His most established strand of research investigates the ways in which colleges and universities build capacity to serve, support, and advocate for undocumented students. His other research interests include critical perspectives on leadership education, trauma-informed practices in higher education, and the phenomenon of religious trauma and its impact on college student identity development.

Shawn Gaines, M.Ed. (he/him), is a management consultant, educator, and mental health professional. His academic background is in organizational communication and higher education administration, with a focus on counseling and helping skills. Shawn is passionate about creating space for folx on the margins. His work has primarily focused on higher education settings and supervising large teams to meet organizational objectives. His passion for Diversity, Equity, and Inclusion (DEI) has been fueled by the love and support he received from his parents. Shawn has trained and supervised large staff, chaired departmental recruitment and selection efforts, and served as a crisis management first responder. An emphasis on social justice and equity has always spurred this blend of experiences, consistently returning to questions about equitable outcomes and diverse representation. Shawn seeks to push the boundaries of what is common/best practice in organizations to prompt real, sustainable change around DEI.

Christy Heaton, Ph.D. (she/her), is the Assistant Vice Chancellor of Student Transitions and Family Engagement at the University of Colorado Denver, where she also serves as a lecturer in the School of Education. Her doctoral research centered around the exploration of undergraduate transgender students' experiences, at institutions of higher education in the south. Other areas of focus include college student transition, first-generation student support, leadership development, and community building. Dr. Heaton spent a decade at the University of New Orleans, focusing on orientation, transition, and retention.

Melvin (Jai) Jackson, Ph.D. (he/him), is a dedicated educator, researcher, and advocate for diversity, equity, and inclusion in higher education. With a passion for empowering individuals and fostering inclusive environments, Jai has significantly contributed to educational leadership. His research contributions span adult and lifelong education, focusing on the experiences of adult learners and issues related to race and diversity within higher education. Jai has been instrumental in higher education administration in areas impacting students, faculty, and staff and has led grant writing and research projects within the field. Driven by a passion for equity and access in education, Jai's professional journey exemplifies his commitment to making a positive impact in the lives of stakeholders and communities.

Jeremy Lane, Ed.D. (he/him), earned his undergraduate degree from Kentucky State University and an Ed.D. from the University of Houston in Educational Leadership, with an emphasis on Special Populations. His doctoral research focused on the scholastic achievements of Early College High School graduates, specifically examining the college readiness rates of students from underrepresented minority populations. He has led university admission teams, developed institutional admission policies, and consulted chief enrollment officers on their new student enrollment and marketing strategies. As a first-generation college graduate, he believes in the effectiveness of college advising and the value of student-centered higher education initiatives. In his spare time, he enjoys visiting museums, watching documentaries, and spending time with his wife and their toddler children.

Kevin Lewis, M.S.Ed. (he/him), is a passionate educator, facilitator, and community builder committed to fostering belonging and equity in learning spaces. With a background in higher education, nonprofit leadership, and global consulting, Kevin has spent his career empowering students and educators to engage in meaningful conversations about leadership, identity, inclusion, and social change. He has facilitated DEI initiatives and trainings across Australia, Canada, and USA, and consults with organizations on the cultivation of spaces where all individuals feel valued and supported. Based in Detroit, Michigan (Waawiyatanong), he enjoys running, podcasts, and watching RuPaul's Drag Race with his partner and puppy.

Kevin McClain, Ph.D. (he/him), serves as the Director of Academic Excellence at Woodland Community College located in Woodland, California. He earned his Ph.D. in Educational Administration from the University of New Orleans. Dr. McClain has held various roles in higher education across Louisiana and Nebraska. His work is focused on advancing student success and narrowing achievement gaps for young men of color.

Erica Ogburn, Ed.D. (she/her), is a student-centered leader with over a decade of experience in strategic planning and operating extension learning sites, academic and student success services, and retention-based program management. Her expertise lies in implementing high-impact advising case management and supporting the diverse needs of community college and university students to promote student persistence and completion. Currently serving as the Director of College Advising for the College of Business at the University of Houston–Downtown, Dr. Ogburn leads initiatives to enhance retention, persistence, and degree completion. She understands the importance of collaboration, partnering with faculty, department chairs, and deans to meet cohort degree completion goals. Dr. Ogburn ensures access to quality advice and support services for over 4,300 College of Business students.

Dr. Ogburn's career includes roles at Louisiana Tech University, managing an extension site, and as the Academic Success Center Manager. She led a diverse team, increased student awareness of online education, and improved student satisfaction through innovative student support approaches. With a Doctorate in Educational Leadership (Higher Education concentration) and an M.A. in Higher Education Student Affairs, she is dedicated to student success and actively engages in higher education organizations, committees, and national conferences. Dr. Ogburn's dissertation focused on the socialization experiences of African American women in higher education student affairs, providing higher education and industry leaders with support in socializing and retaining African American women.

Nicole Caridad Ralston, Ph.D. (she/her), founded Caridad Consulting to support leaders in accessing more compassion, growth, and integrity in the ways they lead their teams and initiatives. She is an experienced educator and leader with over 15 years of work in higher education, nonprofits, and racial equity consulting across various industries. She has dedicated her career to creating inclusive spaces, particularly for those pushed to the margins. In higher education, Dr. Ralston built an office focused on first-year retention, advised service-learning programs, and developed social justice education cohorts. Her dissertation explored how women of color in higher education navigate the intersection of racism and sexism in leadership roles. As an adjunct professor at The University of New Orleans, she teaches "Diversity in Higher Education." She is passionate about advancing equity, centering shared voice, and supporting leadership development. Outside of academia, she is a mom of twins, actively contributes to her community through the ACLU of Louisiana, provides service as a doula, and shares her love of New Orleans culture on Instagram as @EatenPathNola.

Sonia Ivette Valencia, Ph.D. (she/her/ella), is the Director of the TRIO Scholars Program at the University of California, Irvine, where she leads a federally funded educational access, equity, and retention initiative that serves first-generation, low-income, and disabled students. A data-informed scholar-practitioner, she has overseen advising, programming, budgets, compliance with Department of Education regulations, and staff development across multiple student success programs. Dr. Valencia brings over a decade of experience in higher education, having taught courses in English, Gender Studies, and Feminist Research Methodologies at the University of Texas at San Antonio before moving into administrative leadership. Her research and professional practice focus on Chicanx feminisms, educational equity, and building supportive structures for historically underserved student communities. She earned her Ph.D. in English with an emphasis in Chicanx Feminisms from the University of Texas at San Antonio, her M.A. in English from Georgetown University, and her B.A. in English and Women's Studies from the University of California, Riverside. Through her leadership, teaching, and advocacy, Dr. Valencia is committed to effecting institutional change by challenging systemic barriers to equity and advancing pathways that enable historically marginalized students to thrive and lead.

Acknowledgments

This book has been a labor of love, grounded in the shared belief of advancing leadership and creating greater operational efficiency in higher education.

First, the editors would like to thank the contributors for their insight and wisdom shared throughout the pages of this text. Their willingness to share real-world scenarios, lessons learned, and practical applications has brought infrastructural concepts to life. Your voices have enriched this work and brought its purpose to life.

We would also like to thank those leaders and mentors who have played a formative role in our own professional growth. These individuals have shared their time, perspective, and support throughout our time in the field. In particular, we thank Chris Broadhurst, Ph.D.; Derek Dubose, M.Ed.; Christy Heaton, Ph.D.; Alonzo Flowers, Ph.D.; Alicia Kornowa, Ph.D.; Stephanie Krah, Ph.D.; Dave Meredith, Ph.D.; Matt Moore, Ph.D.; A. Mika Moy, OD; Tony Pace; Tracy Pascua Dea, Ph.D.; Z. Scott, JD; Monica Scott, Ed.D.; L. Michelle Vital, Ph.D.; and Andrea Welch, Ph.D. Their guidance and encouragement have shaped our careers.

Lastly, we want to recognize the learning communities within student affairs, including the National Association of Graduate Admission Professionals (NAGAP), the National Association for College Admissions Counseling (NACAC), and American College Personnel Association. Our colleagues in these leadership development programs have significantly shaped the ideas in this book. We are also grateful for the support provided by our respective institutions, the University of California, Berkeley, and the University of Houston–Downtown.

We extend our sincere appreciation to the current and future leaders in higher education who will engage with this resource to promote operational efficiency within their organizations.

Introduction

Mike Hoffshire and Carlos Gooden

INTRODUCTION

Significant emphasis has been placed on the role of student recruitment and retention in higher education settings. Specifically, higher education administrators have long sought to understand the various functional areas that are integral to student development and experience (e.g., academic advising, student involvement, career services). With offices facing many internal and external challenges (e.g., the COVID-19 pandemic, declining student enrollments, higher levels of accountability), many departmental offices have found success by having established policies, operational guidelines, strategic plans, and data to overcome these barriers.

Unfortunately, most managers are not taught through formal education programs what they most need to know to efficiently operate any given functional area. The purpose of this book is to prepare educational leaders to implement actionable items for greater operational efficiency within higher education settings. As such, the editors have developed a model that includes ten core infrastructure components they believe are necessary to achieve greater operational efficiency.

The Model: The Ten Infrastructural Components

Leaders in higher education are often tasked with a multitude of responsibilities, including supervising staff, developing students, and overseeing day-to-day operations for a unit or a particular set of units, to name a few. However, few individuals possess the knowledge and skills to be an effective leader (Waple, 2006). Often relying on their experiences with former supervisors and organizations, they may find themselves too underprepared and overwhelmed to effectively develop a student-centered, efficient functional unit. More notably, unforeseen environmental factors, such as the COVID-19 pandemic, may require all managers in higher education settings to re-examine and develop new approaches to leading offices. During the pandemic, from the highest levels of communication and collaboration to the development of new policies on handling mail, every function of the industry was disrupted.

The purpose of this book is to prepare educational leaders to take actionable items for operational efficiency within higher education settings. As such, the editors have developed an operationalized model that includes ten core infrastructure components they believe are necessary to achieve the above goals (see Figures I.1 and Table I.1).

The editors believe these components are necessary to create a fully functional, efficient, and student-centered organization while contributing to the overall mission of the institution. Each chapter provides an overview of the component while empowering leaders with practical tips and strategies to utilize within their department, division, or institution.

Fundamental Notions

To understand the importance of these infrastructure components, it is essential to recognize the fundamental notions that inform their development. These core ideas lay the groundwork for how the components are designed to enhance leadership and operational efficiency within higher education.

The Shifting Landscape
First, the editors acknowledge the difficult space in which higher education leaders must operate. A tension often exists between navigating the day-to-day responsibilities of managing a unit and the high-level tasks associated with deliverables and outcome

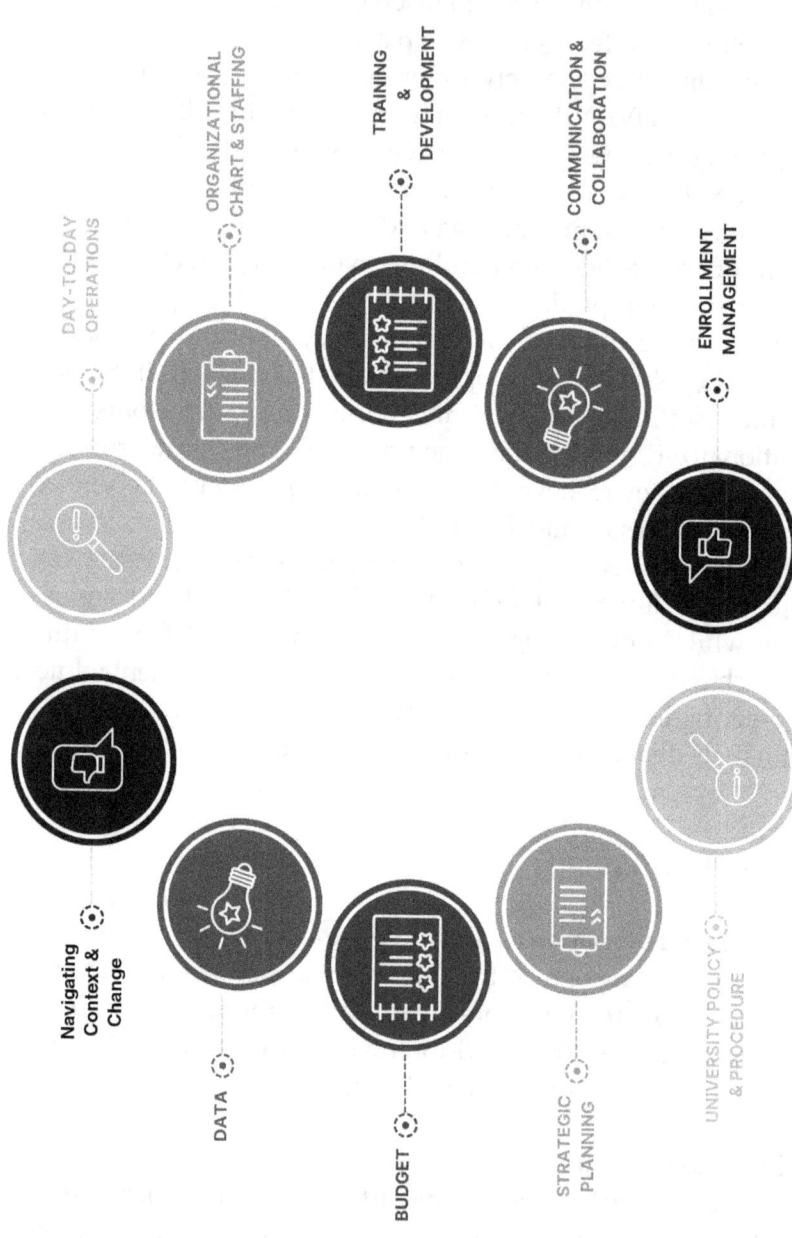

FIGURE I.1 Ten Operational Efficiency Infrastructure Components.

TABLE I.1 Infrastructural Components and Brief Description

Infrastructural Component	Brief Description
Navigating Context & Change	Outlines tools for assessing institutional values and influential factors that inform campus norms.
Data	Describes the importance of and uses for quantitative and qualitative data.
Budget	Focuses on understanding budgets, revenues, and expenses.
Strategic Planning	Provides structure to develop a strategic plan.
University Policy & Procedure	Reviews the importance of understanding federal/state laws and institutional policies.
Day-to-Day Operations	Discusses the importance of and how to develop a daily operations manual.
Organizational Chart & Staffing	Reviews common organizational types, roles, and responsibilities and provides insight on how to manage staff turnover.
Training & Development	Provides strategies for successful onboarding, training, professional development, and performance management of staff.
Communication & Collaboration	Examines the critical role of communication and collaboration.
Enrollment Management	Provides a detailed overview of enrollment management.

measures. By equipping leaders with a framework to navigate priorities, the ten infrastructural components will provide directors with increased capacity to focus on director-level tasks (e.g., supervision, strategic planning, and policy development). With roles clarified, a strong strategic plan and well-documented policies in place, managers can focus on the long-term planning for a well-rounded and efficient unit.

Transfer of Knowledge

The second fundamental notion centers around how leaders learn and develop the skills to maximize operational efficiency. In the transfer of knowledge from manager to employee, it is important to acknowledge that no manager possesses strengths in all aspects of leadership and management. While some leaders possess strengths in many areas, it is assumed that not all leaders are adept at managing every key component needed to lead an effective office. In essence, we learn to lead the way we are led and we manage the way we are managed. Within all leaders, there are opportunities for growth and improvement.

Additionally, there is often an assumption that (our) prior managers have invested in professional development and mentorship to develop employees for future leadership opportunities. An individual's level of preparedness to lead may vary based on prior experiences. Due to limited access to mentorship, professional development, or social capital, all managers may not be not be thoroughly and properly equipped to lead.

Lastly, while some higher education preparation programs have leadership courses built into their curriculum, they often focus on theories and models rather than the practical skill sets needed to oversee a department or division. We believe that colleges and universities generally have not devoted enough systematic attention to leadership development, evaluation, and recognition. All too often, we see colleges and universities either promote from within or appoint the most accomplished scholar in a department to serve as program director or chair. As a result, they are unable to successfully address the wide array of challenges stemming from today's educational environment (e.g., budget shortfalls, declining student enrollment, technological advancements). Consequently, individuals often develop the skills necessary on the job—through observing others and receiving mentorship and professional development opportunities.

Power and Privilege

While the third notion continues to focus on transfer of knowledge from manager to employee, it also affirms that power and privilege structures exist in leadership development and organizations. This fundamental notion systematically examines who receives the training and who has access to receive information related to management and operations efficiency in professional workspaces. The transfer of knowledge that occurs in the workplace is a central part of the social structure that can lead to inequity. As this edited volume was developed, the editors firmly believed that representation of diverse identities, backgrounds, and experiences in leadership matters. It is equally important that rising leaders have opportunities to learn from those that represent their own identities and affinity groups, especially if those identities are underrepresented or from diverse populations. In seeking to address these inequities, the contributors were intentionally curated to include diverse backgrounds and experiences of leadership in action.

Operational Efficiency

The fourth notion encourages leaders to dedicate time to addressing and developing the infrastructure components. Leaders can oftentimes overemphasize achieving their final goals without taking time to appreciate the investments that must be made to build a strong efficient department or division. The infrastructure components developed here assert that goals are best met by achieving operational efficiency. Leaders who tend to these infrastructure components allow them to focus on broader goals and outcomes. Much like a vehicle's performance is measured by its ability to travel from point A to point B, there are other aspects and resources that are needed to keep the car running. In this analogy the infrastructure components are fuel, oil changes, car washes, tune-ups, and tire changes. Without maintenance of these tasks, the car will not be successful in achieving its goal in a sustainable manner. Additionally, the more time invested in maintenance, the less repairs will need to occur over time. In the context of higher education, discussions of progress and success often focus on numbers or deliverables, while insufficient attention is given to the behind-the-scenes infrastructure necessary to achieve broader goals or outcomes.

Applicable and Relevant

These infrastructural components were designed broadly to apply to all leaders and campuses. At a high level, the components are intentionally universal, timeless, and relevant for any department in higher education (while also remaining applicable to all levels of management experience for leaders). Management practices continue to evolve; however, the components were identified and developed to be transferable across institutions while remaining applicable to first-year directors or seasoned managers in higher education.

It is within the context of these guiding notions that the core infrastructure components were developed as a comprehensive guide for managers. As a framework, the components allow for readers to customize for context and according to their unique setting. To ensure broad applicability, it was critical to draw on the collaborative experiences of 13 professionals who have worked at a range of diverse higher education institutions.

Learning Objectives

The goal of this edited volume is to provide a framework (and reference point) for new, mid-level, and senior leaders to create a strong internal infrastructure for any functional area they may oversee. The following learning objectives have been designed to address the needs of managers operating in a fast-paced, evolving environment. By embracing the ten infrastructural components, managers and readers will:

◆ Learn the various infrastructure components necessary to operate any functional area within higher education.
◆ Develop a deeper knowledge and appreciation for the "unseen" tasks needed to achieve optimum operational efficiency within their roles.
◆ Gain practical knowledge and insights from real-world examples to enhance problem-solving and decision-making.
◆ Develop an administrator playbook with specific action items and frameworks to create a foundation for efficient office operations.

Drawing upon experts in the field with a wide range of personal and professional experiences in a variety of settings, each chapter examines one of the ten components. As an administrator playbook, the most unique feature of this text is the actual practical application at the conclusion of each chapter. Readers will leave with tangible practical strategies to apply and execute immediately. With ten steps for operational management, a panel of scholars provide readers with a "golden nugget" they can apply the very next day. This may include a strategy, framework, worksheet, sample queries to request, examples, or questions to ask at the next meeting.

Conclusion

This comprehensive guide equips leaders with the infrastructure and practical applications to successfully lead any department or division in higher education. This playbook is intended to serve as one resource in your toolbox for managing and leading. It is not intended to provide a deep analysis of theory or to replace institution-specific onboarding and training for leaders. Instead, consider how this guide will work in parallel with your leadership training, personal and professional experiences, and the unique context of your institution. As an applicable tool, this playbook complements those resources and enhances prior professional development to focus specifically on the functions of department management and operational efficiency.

Reference

Waple, J. N. (2006). An assessment of skills and competencies necessary for entry-level student affairs work. *NASPA Journal, 43*(1), 1–17.

1

Navigating Context and Change

Carlos Gooden and Mike Hoffshire

INTRODUCTION

This chapter explores the foundational elements required to lead and manage within higher education institutions. First, professionals must engage in deep introspection to clarify their values and leadership identity. Second, they must assess the unique dynamics of their institution, including policies, culture, and internal power structures. Only by understanding both the internal self and external context can leaders implement meaningful and sustained change. With these two layers—self-knowledge and institutional understanding—leaders are positioned to engage in effective change management. Alternatively, failure to engage in these reflective processes can hinder one's ability to lead effectively. As such, the authors conclude this chapter with a review of common change management theories.

The ten infrastructure components discussed in this book serve as a guide to navigating these complexities. As a first component, the rules of engagement within an institution—both formal and informal—ground leaders in principles that ultimately inform all decision-making. The order of operations of the infrastructure components is flexible and can be switched or changed. Regardless of the order of infrastructure components, assessing how to navigate contexts will likely always emerge as a natural starting point. Indeed, honing in on this exercise significantly informs strategic approaches to the other nine infrastructure components for operational efficiency (see the Appendix).

Know Thyself

The first step in navigating institutional cultures and managing change requires a foundational step in self-awareness. Leaders must critically examine their values, strengths, and professional identity to understand how these elements influence their approach to navigating campus environments. Regardless of institutional type, organizational culture, or the internal politics, the first and most essential step in this process is to *know thyself*. This increased self-awareness forms the foundation of effective leadership in decision-making, personal growth and development, improved communication, and conflict resolution. Benefits of heightened self-awareness include:

- Recognizing gaps between one's current skills and the expectations of their professional role.
- Using an understanding of one's professional identity and core values serves as a compass during organizational change or conflict. When grounded in values, leaders can respond with greater clarity and confidence.
- Knowing when and how to bring one's authentic self to work—essential for navigating environments where authenticity may be supported or must be strategically withheld.

Engaging in exercises that heighten self-awareness such as career mapping, self-assessments tools (e.g., CliftonStrengths) and values inventories can provide insights into one's professional identity. While approaching an exercise of introspection can be overwhelming, one starting point is to reflect on five questions:

1. What do I know?
2. What do I believe?
3. What can I do?
4. What do I want to be?
5. How will I influence students?

This exercise, presented in Dr. Gooden's capstone course at the University of Toledo, allowed him to engage in self-reflection on how he arrived at the profession, helped articulate his values and skills, and directed him to core values that would guide him throughout his career. To further ground his responses and shape his professional identity, he needed to present artifacts to support his responses. Today, these values guide his assessments on institutional fit and help ground him in purpose and meaning in his work. This practical application proved to be a valuable exercise that he now recommends all aspiring leaders define for themselves.

Indeed, this kind of personal inventory is an ongoing practice that should be conducted regularly throughout one's professional career. Many inventory assessments assert that our values and characteristics or even strengths are not static. As individuals grow and accumulate experiences, our perspectives change. As such, it is important that professionals engage with these questions, inventories, and values assessments consistently.

By engaging in this self-exploration exercise, one can truly begin to have transformative internal conversations, on how to seek information regarding people and processes. Moreover, the results of a personal inventory assessment informs how to approach the next step of assessing campus culture.

Navigating Context: Campus Culture

Navigating campus culture and climate requires an integrative approach that considers both professional values and institutional context. The culture within higher education institutions is unique and specific and encompasses the beliefs, customs, and practices within the environment. The dynamics of a campus are intricately complex and define how individuals and groups interact within the environment. In the context of culture, effective leadership requires understanding the people and the processes that drive the institution. Furthermore, institutions are shaped by historical, political, social, and economic factors that inform and influence every aspect of how an institution functions. Together, these elements form a culture that establishes ways of working and sets the tone for accomplishing goals. A comprehensive understanding of campus culture not only elevates individual leadership but also contributes to the broader mission of the institution.

To know the campus requires an understanding of its culture and climate, since both shape the way an institution functions. More specifically, campus culture reflects shared patterns of behavior, norms, and expectations that guide the rules of engagement (Quinn & Thakor, 2018). Often, this culture shapes how decisions are made within the community and describes how members within the organization interact. Campus culture norms can manifest as both formal and informal and simultaneously be visible and invisible. In examining campus culture, leaders may look to the following elements:

- **Climate**: What are the current perceptions, attitudes, and emotional tones felt by members of the campus community?
- **Patterns and behaviors**: How are meetings conducted? Who speaks, who listens, and how are decisions made?
- **Protocols and traditions**: What are the routine practices or events grounded in the institution's history?
- **Socialization**: How are new faculty, students, and staff introduced to expectations and campus-specific behaviors?

♦ **Politics and bureaucracy**: What cultural or policy-based undercurrents influence decision-making?

As a starting point for learning and navigating campus culture, managers can first start by posing the following questions:

1. What is the mission of the institution?
2. What is the personality of your campus?
3. What are the campus politics that inform how work is approached at the institution?
4. What are the rules of engagement?
5. How are decisions made in this environment?
6. What are your resources? Who are your allies?
7. What is the historical context of your institution on social and political themes?
8. What is the historical context of your department and the individual that worked in this position before you?

Ultimately, assessing campus culture informs managers of their ability (or authority) to challenge norms. Furthermore, it can help them identify best approaches to navigating within established structures. Administrators must understand these dynamics to foster effective collaboration and to advance department goals.

Navigating Change

As higher educational professionals and leaders, we have become accustomed to the concept of change. Whether that be navigating complex organizational structures and competing priorities, assisting with student crises, or creating new programs and services despite impending institutional and state budget cuts, professionals are being asked to remain adaptable in an ever-changing environment. For the purpose of this book, we define change as a constant process that allows organizations to adapt to new technologies, methodologies, and societal demands. It can be planned (e.g., a shift in reporting structure) or unplanned (e.g., the COVID-19 pandemic) and is often the result of the organization responding to internal or external pressures and changing environments.

The act of reviewing organizational structure or components can be disruptive, especially for those who are not ready. Consider these three key drivers that impact change readiness (Combe, 2014):

- **Cultural readiness**: the degree of alignment between cultural norms and the proposed change.
- **Commitment readiness**: the degree of resolve and ability of the organization—through its leaders at all levels—to see the change through to successful and sustainable completion within the organization's overall strategic agenda.
- **Capacity readiness**: the degree to which the organization can leverage supportive work processes, historical knowledge and experience, current knowledge, skills and abilities, and resources to aid in successful implementation and sustainability of the change.

Before embarking on a change, leaders should first examine why they are about to embark on the process, why it is needed, how best to approach it, and determine the intended results. While there is no exact method or formula for managing change, there are a number of theories that can be utilized to assist organizations. As leaders, we understand the impact the impending change will have not only on the technical side (policies, procedures, reporting structures, etc.) but also on individuals (educators). The models described below are not meant to be an exhaustive list of all change management theories and models, but rather a few that the editors have found to be most useful in describing and navigating change.

Lee Bolman and Terrence Deal's Four Framework Approach

Often utilized as a leadership model, Bolman and Deal's model allows leaders at all levels to view a challenging situation or a change through one of four different perspectives to analyze and propose solutions: structural, human resource, political, and symbolic. These frames allow leaders to better understand situations and adapt to changing conditions and contexts (Bolman & Deal, 1991).

The structural frame encourages leaders to focus on how to change and is mainly task-orientated. It relies on a strong chain of command while communicating clear and measurable goals, identifying tasks and reporting lines, agreeing to deadlines, and creating systems and procedures. Such an approach requires knowledge that a change is imminent. The human resource frame places the emphasis on an individual's needs, primarily focusing on giving employees power and opportunity to learn and perform their job well. This framework assumes that the organization will succeed, regardless of any change, if everyone's needs within the organization are met. The third frame, political, places emphasis on the understanding that individuals and interest groups within an organization are sometimes in conflict with one another. Leaders who help others to understand resource guarding and coalition building are utilizing this framework. Lastly, the symbolic frame addresses employees' needs for a greater sense of purpose in their work. By creating a unifying vision, individuals can have a better understanding of the need for change and their role in facilitating it. Rather than utilize a single framework, Bolman and Deal advocate for the adoption of a multi-frame perspective.

Adrianna Kezar's Multiple Change Perspective Approach

A national expert and leader on change and leadership in higher education, Adrianna Kezar's (2018) research furthered the framework created by Bolman and Deal. In supporting policymakers, change agents, and scholars, Kezar conceptualized six perspectives about why and how change occurs. These include scientific management (similar to structural), evolutionary, social cognition, cultural (similar to symbolic), political, and institutional. The scientific management perspective views change as primarily occurring from the top-down, driven by leaders who see a need for change and develop and provide incentives for meeting goals.

An evolutionary change perspective centers the role of the external context influencing organizational change. In higher education, examples could include the implementation of new technologies within a unit or department. Utilizing Kezar's third perspective, social cognition, change can only be achieved when the thought process of individuals shift. Fourth, the cultural perspective argues that the organizational culture is always changing in response to the environment. It relies heavily on the belief that values can influence an organization's functioning both formally and informally. A political perspective focuses on the identity and ideology of the organization and views change as a natural outcome of conflict and negotiation. Finally, an institutional perspective considers the larger context of change in higher education. Examples could include the actions of state governments or responses to dwindling budgets and resources. Kezar believed that change was purposeful and driven internally by leaders in organizations. She also advocated for the use of multiple perspectives. However, she acknowledges that the six change perspectives do not prescribe specific actions to achieve change within an organization.

The Prosci ADKAR® Model

Founded in 1994, Prosci assists organizations in effective and successful change management. Developed by founder Jeff Hiatt of Prosci, the ADKAR® model (see Figure 1.1) assists leaders with focusing on employee thoughts and behaviors rather than processes, procedures, and outcomes of an intended change. ADKAR® is an acronym for the five outcomes an individual needs to achieve for a change to be successful: Awareness, Desire, Knowledge, Ability, and Reinforcement (Ball, 2024). These strategies are designed to assist leaders with empowering their employees to embrace a new mindset and identify the essential actions that will foster transformation. First, leaders should increase awareness and transparency surrounding the need for change (Awareness). Within a higher education setting, this can occur through the use of one-on-one meetings or staff meetings. Second, leaders should encourage individuals to participate and support the change (Desire). An example may be for leaders to provide opportunities to staff for feedback and involvement.

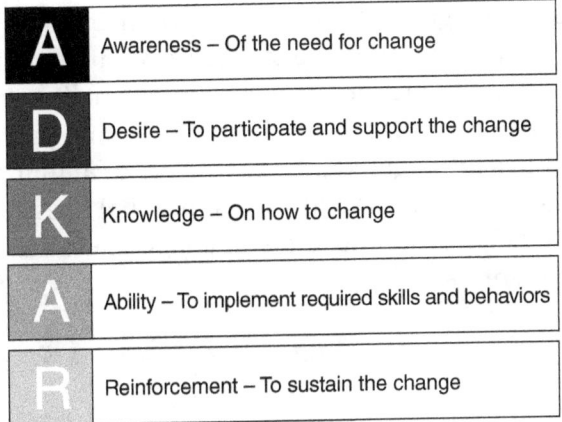

FIGURE 1.1 Prosci ADKAR® Model.

Helping individuals to understand how and why they will benefit from the change is an important aspect of this component. Third, leaders should provide the knowledge of how to change as well as the ability to implement the required skills and behaviors for the change to occur (Knowledge and Ability). Employees within an organization should have the opportunity to learn through training and professional development as well as possess autonomy in their role. Finally, leaders should reinforce attitudes and behaviors to sustain the desired change (Reinforce). Examples could include small tokens of acknowledgment and/or promotional opportunities. The ADKAR® model ensures that there is a focus on what is required to prepare, equip, and support individuals to adopt changes within an organization. However, it is important to note that while ADKAR® is a valuable tool, it does not provide a comprehensive approach, process, and set of tools for managing change at the organizational level.

Conclusion

Understanding one's self and campus culture is foundational to effective leadership in higher education. By prioritizing self-awareness and strategic assessments, managers are best positioned to navigate the complexities of their roles with confidence. Engaging with the practical applications outlined in this chapter can lead to higher levels of job satisfaction and greater administrative operational efficiency. This first infrastructure component has highlighted the importance of aligning personal and professional values within institutional contexts. Doing so fosters a culture that positions managers and teams to best support students.

References

Ball, K. (2024). *The ADKAR advantage: Your new lens for successful change.* Self-published.

Bolman, L.G. & Deal, T.E. (1991). *Reframing organizations.* Jossey-Bass.

Combe, M. (2014). *Change agility: Readiness for strategy implementation* [White paper]. Project Management Institute.

Kezar, A. (2018). *How colleges change: Understanding, leading, and enacting change.* Routledge.

Quinn, R.E. & Thakor, A.V. (2018). Creating a purpose-driven organization: How to get employees to bring their smarts and energy to work. *Harvard Business Review*, https://apps.olin.wustl.edu/faculty/thakor/Website%20Papers/CreatingPurposeDrivenOrganization_2018-06.pdf

Appendix

Navigating Context and Campus Culture Within the Ten Infrastructural Components

Infrastructure Component	Self-Assessment	Campus Culture
Context and Change	How do you present yourself as a professional? As a supervisor?	How are you allowed to present as a professional? As a supervisor?

Infrastructure Component	Self-Assessment	Campus Culture
Data	How do you best process information for decision-making, quantitatively or qualitatively?	How is data collected at your institution? What is the data culture at your institution?
Budget	What is your level of comfort with developing and managing budgets? How confident are you in your ability to advocate for resources?	What level of influence do you have in the budget development process? What are the levels of bureaucracy that inform spending? Is there competition for resources?
Strategic Planning	At what steps of the strategic planning process are you adept? With what steps do you need assistance?	What is the mission of your institution and department? How do you situate your purpose within the context of the institution, the local context, and national landscape?
University Policy & Procedure	How familiar are you with your institution's policy and procedure?	What are the institutional policies that determine the parameters? What are the unwritten rules that guide behaviors? Why do certain policies exist?
Day-to-Day Operations	What is your management style? What type of work/office culture do you want to create for colleagues?	What institutional policies exist that impact your work at the department level?
Organizational Chart & Staffing	Who are your professional mentors? What did they teach you?	What is the career ladder program at your institution?
Training & Development	How do you support career growth and advocate for others?	What resources does the institution have to support ongoing professional development?
Communication & Collaboration	What are your preferred methods of communication? How do you best collaborate with others?	What communication and collaboration licenses and software are available to staff?

(continued)

Infrastructure Component	Self-Assessment	Campus Culture
Enrollment Management	How do you and your office impact the student experience?	Is enrollment management centralized or decentralized? Is there a written strategic enrollment management plan? What is the involvement level of campus departments?

2

Harnessing and Leveraging Data as a Leader in Higher Education

Erica Ogburn and Jeremy Lane

INTRODUCTION

The use of data in higher education has long standing significance and implications for leaders on campus. In an era of increased accountability and evolving funding models (Chapter 3), data has emerged as a necessary tool for leaders. From enhancing student engagement to optimizing institutional operations, the ability to collect and interpret data is crucial for making informed decisions that impact students, faculty, staff, and institutional success.

As a professional undertaking the job search, you began harnessing campus data to inform your decision to apply, interview, and accept your current role. Whether it was institutional endowment, the current enrollment, or student and faculty climate surveys, these qualitative and quantitative data points provided additional insight into your decision-making processes. These tools ultimately helped you to make a decision regarding fit. In Chapter 1, tools were provided for assessing a campus climate and culture.

As the second infrastructure component, data is intentionally positioned as an underpinning priority for leaders due to its strong connections to the other infrastructure components. Inherently, it becomes easy to conceptualize the ways data impacts important elements such as budget, strategic planning, and even recruitment and retention. By building a strong data culture within a unit, managers can become adept storytellers who influence stakeholders and advance institutional goals. This chapter explores models for harnessing data and its critical role in higher education by further delving into its uses, applications, and reviewing frameworks necessary for leveraging data effectively.

Purpose of Data

The primary purpose of data is to establish a foundation for more effective organizational efficiency and success. Indeed, there are strong connections between data and decision-making. Data tells a story on a micro and macro level. The most effective managers harness data to draw strong connections between data and decision-making.

Data at the Micro Level

On a micro level, data application has several impacts on a department's operational efficiency. Examples of data that may be used at a micro level to inform decisions may include student interactions, events, and course evaluations. By effectively harnessing the broad uses of data, leaders will be able to achieve some of the following functionalities in their daily roles:

- Map data metrics to strategic objectives of the institution
- Advocate for resource allocation and strategic support
- Evaluate staff performance and progress
- Monitor departmental key performance indicators
- Engage stakeholders

- Track progress toward mission and goals
- Provide training and serve as a professional development tool
- Achieve accreditation standards
- Secure grants and funding for key initiatives
- Enhance student engagement

We provide three examples to operationalize these bullet points. In campus safety, harnessing data can mean using event RSVP data to identify security staffing levels at an upcoming campus concert. For department chairs, applying data means understanding enrollment and retention numbers to plan course loads (the number of classes offered and setting capacity sizes) to ensure there are enough classes to meet demands. The Business Affairs Office will monitor data to understand enrollment headcount and student credit hours to forecast budgeting models and projections for revenue.

Data at a Macro Level

Additionally, managers can drive strategies to accomplish a wide range of goals that are needed in higher education. Examples include metrics that inform institutional sustainability and decision-making often in the context of student enrollment, persistence, engagement, and graduation rates. At a macro level, data has led organizations through significant milestones of change and assessment. Managers may use data at the macro level for:

- Performance-based budgeting
- Institutional strategic planning
- Student engagement and experience at an institutional level
- Retention of students
- Cost-of-living salary increases
- Enrollment projections
- Academic program offerings
- Accreditation

For example, enrollment managers frequently uses Western Interstate Commision for Higher Education (WICHE) data to analyze birth rates and project college enrollment rates 18–20 years into the future. This data helps states and institutional leaders anticipate potential growth of students on campus (increase) or begin developing contingency plans if fewer students are expected on campus. These data points have a direct implication on tuition revenue, services, and resources needed.

Indeed, data is the fabric that interconnects all leaders in higher education. As a manager, you've likely learned that every decision made has some form of data and analysis at its core. Therefore, a firm grasp on data involves an understanding of what data is relevant to your unit and how to obtain it. This chapter will outline a five-step framework for leaders to apply. These key steps focus not only on understanding what data is needed, but also knowing how to acquire and apply it effectively while providing guidance for dissemination to stakeholders.

A Framework for Harnessing Data: Business Intelligence Lifecycle

Conceptualizing a starting point for leveraging data is crucial, but can also be overwhelming. With an infinite amount of data points available, understanding what questions to ask to obtain the correct data needed can be a challenging task. Additionally, unclear objectives or uncertainty on where to source data may lead to mistakes or time wasted.

To create efficiency for the data collection process, this chapter takes an interdisciplinary approach to harnessing data through lessons from the business industry. The business discipline has a long-standing history of using data to glean insights and turning them into meaningful action to impact outcomes for organizations. With developments in technology, a newer discipline has emerged known as Business Intelligence. The five-phase model of the business intelligence cycle provides a concise framework for breaking down a complex topic, such as data, and making it manageable for leaders in higher education (Bartes, 2013). The steps to strategic data application are:

1. Task Definition
2. Data Collection
3. Information Processing and Storing
4. Analyze and Interpret
5. Dissemination

By organizing the harnessing of data into these five steps, a linear process is created while avoiding mistakes. Eager managers, looking to make an immediate impact, may have an impulse to start collecting data immediately. However, the first step of the five-phase model requires approaching data collection by clearly identifying the questions (or problems) the data is intended to address.

Step 1: Task Definition
Before collecting data, you need to identify the questions you want to answer to guide your query development. By narrowing your objective and focusing on key uses and purposes, you can avoid gathering excessive information. After all, collecting too many data points creates challenges when managing, organizing, and analyzing/interpreting. As a first step, task definition enables managers to intentionally and strategically frame the process for approaching data gathering, ensuring they ask the right questions for accurate and effective data collection. Some key questions that support task definition are:

♦ What is the core function of your department?
♦ What are the strategies aimed to achieve these goals?
♦ What are you attempting to measure?
♦ How do you track progress?
♦ Are you monitoring these metrics on a daily, weekly, monthly, term-by-term or annual basis?

Defining the task (or objective) will serve as the foundation for collecting the appropriate data needed for your inquiry. At a high level, data can reflect a functional overview of the unit. Data collected with this task serves the purpose of describing the function and mission of the department. On a departmental level, data is collected to provide a snapshot of performance metrics in the environment. These data points are referred to as "key performance metrics" and serve the purpose of informing strategy. The Appendix expands on this by providing sample queries for key performance metrics in an Admissions context.

Step 2: Data Collection

The second phase of harnessing data includes having a robust data collection process to ensure that managers are aware of their resources for collecting data and knowing the process for obtaining the data at your institution. To begin data collection as a manager, begin by understanding the two primary sources for data collection. These two primary sources, or methodologies, for data collection are known as quantitative data and qualitative data. Differentiating the two methodologies informs managers where to seek and collect data.

The data collection process often involves examining qualitative and quantitative sources for the information you need to arrive at decisions. Differentiating between the two organizes the data collection process into two separate, but equal, mindsets. Examples of quantitative data may include databases such as the National Center for Education Statistics, Common Data Sets, or the National Student Clearinghouse. Examples of qualitative data may include campus student satisfaction surveys, campus climate surveys, or performance reviews. Whereas quantitative data may reveal numerical data (e.g., head counts), qualitative data provides insights into behaviors or attitudes (e.g., engagement or satisfaction).

Oftentimes, data collection is where most challenges are found in the five-step process. From data silos, lack of resources, competing institutional priorities, or misinterpretations of definitions, there are a number of errors that can occur when working with data. These challenges cannot be completely avoided, but the following principles and best practices can guide managers by ensuring the data request is:

- ♦ **Accurate:** Data should be collected using institutionally approved request procedures and verified data sources (e.g.,

Institutional Research (IR) or intake forms) and must reflect campus-specific definitions, acronyms, and institution-specific terminology.
- **Complete**: Requests should include a broad range of variables to provide a holistic view of metrics presented.
- **Timely**: Data points should reflect current conditions and connections to enable relevant decision-making.
- **Contextualized**: It is essential to understand key definitions and the culture of acronyms (e.g., "returning student," "former student," or "stop-out"), as well as special cohort designations.
- **Ethical**: Data use must adhere to governing privacy laws and ethical standards such as the Family Education Rights and Privacy Act (FERPA), or Institutional Review Board (IRB) protocols.

One final consideration is timeliness. Establish how often the data needs to be updated and examined to serve its purpose (e.g., daily, weekly, monthly, by term, or annually). Simultaneously, timeliness refers to the amount of time it may take to get the data back. Some requests may take seconds while others may be two weeks or longer. With these best practices in mind, you are likely to achieve the most accurate data that is useful and aligned with institutional needs.

Step 3: Information Processing and Storing

The third phase of the data application process involves developing systems to organize and store the collected data within your unit. As a starting point, your institution will often have licenses, software, and platforms provided to you for data requests and storing. Offices such as the Registrar and IR may depend on broad databases known as Student Information Systems (SIS) including Banner or PeopleSoft. These provide reliable data points to draw pertinent queries. Other examples of databases that contain student data for queries may include Navigate360, Degree Works, Hobson Starfish, or your campus customer relationship management (CRM) platform. Using these data systems, IR may create a process and mechanisms for requesting data. While it is important for managers to become aware of such processes and procedures, it is duly important to also become familiar with institutional terminology, definitions, acronyms, and timelines.

A final step of information processing is having a plan for organizing and storing data. For example, will files and data be archived on a shared drive that can only be accessed on campus? Is there a cloud-based tool (e.g., Microsoft Teams, iCloud, Google Suite) or licensed tool, (e.g., Microsoft Excel or Access) identified as the central organizing method? Finally, managers must be prepared to answer the following question regarding security and access: What are the rules of sharing data and ensuring security of sensitive student information? Regardless of method or platform used for storing, preparation and planning for data file management is paramount to operational efficiency in the data process.

Step 4: Analyze and Interpret

The fourth step involves interpreting the data to extract insights from the larger parts of data sets. Data interpretation allows organizational improvements to be based on evidence, rather than anecdotal experience. Analyzing data requires drawing connections to examine the internal and external landscape.

This proactive approach enables leaders to examine data to:

- Draw connections between strategies and outcomes
- Clarify and illuminate a unit's performance
- Identify trends and patterns
- Anticipate potential challenges and address them
- Analyze the data to inform action
- Assess quality and effectiveness of strategies

More importantly, analyzing data elements involves reviewing several data elements to draw connections between two or more strategies. Data elements may include budget spending, student engagement, student outcomes, or return on investment calculations. For example, a director may connect the total budget spent to the number of students served to determine cost per student. Based on the trends and findings among these data elements, leaders can deduce, or induce, conclusions to develop strategies.

Step 5: Disseminate
By interpreting the data for trends and insights, managers can draw tangible outcomes, inform decisions, create proposals, and develop their meetings and agendas (with their team, peers, or supervisor). This leads to the fifth and final stage of the business life cycle which is disseminating, or sharing the findings with stakeholders in clear and actionable formats.

First, consider when there are opportunities to implement change, reassess policies, and cultivate long-term strategies. Data is truly the baseline and reference point for conveying important information within and across teams. This step has affectionately become known as storytelling and is a critical skill for managers in higher education to develop. Storytelling has been the most effective way of generating interest and feedback from staff and senior leadership. Data, when presented as a compelling narrative, has the power to engage and inspire. There are two considerations when disseminating data.

The first consideration involves sharing the conclusions and findings in a way that resonates with stakeholders. This may involve presenting the same data in various formats based on audience so that it is clear. The effective ways to present data to staff and senior leadership are as follows:

- Understanding the difference in audience and the importance of different delivery based on your audience
- Simplifying complex data through the use of visuals
- Having such an understanding of the data, that it can be used to tell a story
- Being consistent and clear, and
- Focusing on recommendations and solutions versus illuminating the problem

A second consideration in disseminating data involves selecting the medium or vehicle for conveying the narrative. Visual tools, such as charts that display year-over-year performance metrics, assist with effective storytelling by providing a visual representation to enhance dialogue. For team-based presentations the data dissemination may come in the form of weekly meeting agendas or written reports. When the same data is presented to institutional leadership, the data may be more abridged and accompanied by an executive summary. The presentation of the data influences the audience's engagement with these stories and makes the work meaningful and impactful.

Although last, this stage truly reflects the collective efforts and labor of the first four steps. The dissemination of data allows managers to celebrate victories by highlighting wins and successes within the department. Storytelling through data is a strategy to express transparency, create trust, and request buy-in from internal and external audiences.

Putting It All Together

By adopting frameworks like the five-phase model of the intelligence cycle, leaders can operationalize big data projects into smaller, more workable parts. Conceptualizing these five steps in action, let's consider an admissions office meeting with the university's president to review status updates on enrollment. The meeting is requested because there are 30 days left until the first day of classes begin, but 100 more new students are needed to meet the new student enrollment goal. In this example, the admissions manager is expected to discuss the current numbers in the context of the upcoming deadline.

The manager in admissions has collected the data to track applications and enrollment over time. This information informs the manager if the strategies of outreach, marketing, and campus visit programs are working to attract, recruit, and enroll students.

Task Definition

The first step involves collecting functional data to describe the overall purpose of the organization and using this information for modeling to draw connections over time. In this case, the manager is looking to answer what data best exhibits the mission to attract, admit, and enroll students. The manager is asking for a query that demonstrates the number of applications, admittances, and enrolled students over the past two to three years. At a more granular level, data can be further analyzed by major, geography, age, student type, race, or gender for further analyses.

Data Collection

The data needed for this analysis is housed in two systems: CRM or the SIS. For the manager, the data collection process will involve narrowing a set of data points from a larger data set. A manager would identify the appropriate data representative (in Enrollment Management or Institutional Research) to become familiar with the data definitions and formal ways of submitting data requests. To draw stronger conclusions from this large application data set, the data is collected on a month-to-month basis and evaluated by term.

Information Processing and Storing

To prepare for this meeting is easy because the data needed to answer questions is accessible within the department and organized accordingly. Internal tracking occurs in Microsoft Excel or Microsoft Teams on a monthly basis to track how many students apply and enroll each month. The folder is titled Data and contains sub-folders that include each term for appropriate tracking.

The storing and organization plan has been maintained, making it easy to track student admission and enrollment trends over time.

Analyze

If your institution is concerned about meeting numbers because 100 more students are needed to meet the goal and there are only 30 days left until classes begin, you currently have the archival data to present in your meeting. Since this data has been efficiently maintained and monitored consistently over the years, a trend analysis of students who have enrolled 30 days prior to the term can be accessed and assessed. By looking at the August data in the previous three to five years, you may learn that an average of 200 students have historically enrolled in the month of August. While this is one informational data point, and not comprehensive, it is a finding that will be valuable to institutional leaders.

Disseminate

In a meeting with the institution's president, it may not be a best practice to open the full file with all of the data presented in rows and columns. Instead, parse out the relevant data points on a Word document or PowerPoint where it can be reviewed and summarized in a quick and easily digestible chart.

Through this five-step process, managers are equipped to harness data for informed decision-making and strategic planning. To achieve operational efficiency, leaders must develop the outlined skills to interpret data, understand trends and patterns, and effectively communicate findings. Based on the author's experiences, these practices lead to data-driven decision-making, strategic planning, and better resource allocation. Data-driven decision-making is the central goal for new leaders, challenging traditional norms that may resist these practices.

Conclusion

As underscored in this chapter, data has the power to make or break a manager's experience by enabling leaders to make informed decisions, demonstrate accountability, and become effective storytellers and advocates for their department. In an era of rapid change, increased complexity, and heightened accountability, data has truly emerged as a central resource (and starting point) for leaders seeking operational efficiency. Collectively, data assessments position institutional leadership to make long-term decisions that ultimately support students.

From increasing fundraising efforts to enhancing student engagement, the ability to collect, analyze, and effectively disseminate data is critical for driving evidence-based decision-making. As the dynamic landscape of higher education changes, a commitment to data-driven practices will ensure that managers remain responsive and efficient. This chapter has explored the transformative potential of data for managers in higher education and provided a roadmap for how administrators can harness this data in their daily work. Moreover, the chapter outlined a five-step framework of harnessing data to create a transformative and robust data culture. As the second component, the principles of harnessing data can be used as a lens to inform the subsequent infrastructure components. The most clear and inherent implication of data application can be found in the next chapter that addresses budgeting as a manager in higher education.

Reference

Bartes, F. (2013). Five-phase model of the intelligence cycle of competitive intelligence. *Acta Universitatis Agriculturae et Silviculturae Mendelianae Brunensis, 61*(2), 283–288.

Appendix

Sample Queries a Manager in Admissions May Collect

- Enrollment trends (term by term, 3-year, 5-year)
    - Segmented by population and/or demographics
- Inquiries and prospects
- Applications
- Admits
- Deposits
- Enrolled

- Campus tour registrations and attendees
- Outreach efforts
  - High school visit
  - Community college events
  - College fair activity
- Social media engagement
- Customer service engagement (e.g., emails, phone calls, forms submitted)
- Top feeder schools
- Scholarship awarding
- Financial aid applications
- Housing deposits
- Orientation registrations

3

Aligning Resources: Understanding the Budget Process

Emily Erwin

INTRODUCTION

Jon McGee (2016) succinctly stated, "Colleges and universities today must be understood for what they are: large-scale business enterprises" (p. 5). While this sentiment is relevant, it must be tempered with an understanding of higher education's core mission and values. As higher education institutions grapple with budget shortfalls (Nietzel & Ambrose, 2024), modern higher education leaders must balance a focus on the financial bottom line with sensitivity toward their institution's cultural norms and student success. Essentially, an institution needs enough money to offer quality programs and services, while being mindful of spending to remain sustainable. This balancing act requires leaders at all levels within higher education institutions to understand:

- How their departments contribute to the overall revenue and expense of the institution,
- The budgeting process and budget models,
- Best practices on advocating for resources to decision-makers in the budget request process.

It is a tall order, but one that can be accomplished with some basic knowledge of the institutional budget process and institutional goals, as well as some strategies for advocating for resources.

Understanding Budgets, Revenues, and Expenses

All universities and colleges have budgets. Budgets are simply plans that outline expected or realized revenues and expenses. Revenue is the money the institution expects to receive/receives (from the state, from tuition charges to students, from grants, or from wealthy donors). Expenses represent the money the institution expects to spend/spends (on salaries/related benefits, electricity, building maintenance, technology, travel, supplies, etc.). Ideally, expenditures should be less than or equal to revenues.

It is important for leaders at all levels to understand the most common kinds of revenue and expenses in higher education and within their own departments and units. This knowledge is instrumental in having resource allocation discussions with campus leaders and subordinates. This knowledge also provides leaders with an understanding of the fiscal constraints inherent in operating an institution.

The National Association of College and University Business Officers (NACUBO) provides guidance on financial management and reporting for institutions throughout the United States. For most financial officers, NACUBO is considered the primary authority on how to account for and report revenues and expenditures. In addition, most state agencies require public colleges and universities to report their revenues and expenditures in accordance with NACUBO reporting standards, with some state-to-state variation. Therefore, budgets are generally organized following the NACUBO reporting schema, with slight variations to account for local nuances.

Revenue

Revenues are the incoming funds into the institution that are recorded and reported based upon their source. They are often divided into two broad categories – restricted and unrestricted. Restricted revenues include grants, philanthropy, monies generated from auxiliary enterprises (such as the food sold to students in the cafeteria or the school-branded T-shirts sold within the campus bookstore), and monies from local or state entities that are earmarked for specific purposes. Unrestricted revenues include monies from the tuition and fees charged to students, as well as state and local appropriations provided for general operating expenses.

As the names imply, restricted revenues can only be used to pay for those items, services, and salaries that fall within the parameters of the revenue. For instance, money received as part of a grant cannot be spent on items, services, or salaries that are outside the scope of the grant. In contrast, unrestricted revenues often become part of a general fund and are used to operate the institution. These funds are then distributed to departments through the institution's budgeting process. Distinguishing the difference between revenues and their parameters is important for leaders to understand. For example, an overall increase in the budget may not always mean an increase in unrestricted funds. Likewise, additional revenues generated by a specific department or unit may not always return to that department or unit for expenditure.

Expenditures

Whereas revenue accounts for the incoming funds into the institution, expenditures are the outgoing funds from the department or institution to support operations. Typically, expenditures are categorized by object, such as salaries, fringe benefits, travel, operating services, supplies, professional services, debt services, interagency transfers, and major repairs. For most departments and units, most expenditures by object are spent on salaries and fringe benefits. Higher education is an intensely people-focused enterprise and thus the bulk of expenditures are for people (employees). This is understandable, but unfortunate during lean financial periods when reductions in force may be necessary because there are very few other object categories to cut in any significant amount.

NACUBO outlines nine general areas of expenditure by function:

Instruction	Research	Public Service
Academic Service/Support	Student Services	Institutional Support
Operation/Maintenance of Plant	Scholarships/ Fellowships	Auxiliary Enterprises

While there are common types of expenditures across higher education institutions, the funding allocated to each expense category may differ depending on the unique mission, priorities, structures, and needs of each individual campus. According to the National Center for Education Statistics (NCES; 2023), instruction (which includes faculty salaries) comprised the largest single expense category at public two-year and four-year institutions, representing 38%–34%, respectively, in 2020–2021. At private two-year and four-year institutions, the largest expense category was a combined category of academic support, student services, and institutional support, comprising 40%–68% of all expenses (NCES, 2023). This data indicates that most colleges and universities spend a significant amount of their funds on instruction and academic support activities. However, given the variability in expenditure spending, a look at the overall mission and institutional type can determine the budgeting priorities for an institution. This is important to understand if you lead a division not primarily associated with such functions. While NACUBO outlines nine general expenditure categories at an institutional level, a list of samples of expenditures often found in departmental budgets can be found in the Appendix.

The Budget Is a Process

Beyond an understanding of revenues and expenditures, leaders must also understand that budgeting is an ongoing and fluid exercise. At the beginning of each fiscal year, the budget is a forecast (often referred to as the "Projected Budget") and as the year progresses the budget slowly moves from being theoretical to actual. Once the fiscal year closes, that fiscal year's budget is then referred to as the "Actual Budget" (no longer the "Projected Budget"). For example, the institution may expect to receive $10 million dollars from the state (in the case of a public institution) and $15 million in tuition revenue. The year's projected budget is then built on the assumption that the institution will have $25 million in revenue to spend. Expenses are then estimated and either increased or decreased commensurate with the estimated amount of revenue.

Midway through the fiscal year, there may be a shortfall. Perhaps the state did not collect as much taxes as it expected to collect, or perhaps the institution did not enroll as many students as it expected to enroll, or the electrical bill was much higher than anticipated. Using the example above, perhaps the institution only collected $10 million (of the projected $15 million) in tuition revenue. In this case, the shortfall has to be accounted for by decreasing the budget midway through the fiscal year by $5 million so as to maintain a balance between revenues and expenses. As a result, either $5 million in expenses has to be cut or an additional $5 million in revenue has to be raised. It is also plausible that the budget may be balanced by a circumstantial change in another budget category. For example, the state could collect more tax revenue than anticipated, the institution could enroll more students than expected, or the electrical bill could be lower than anticipated. In this case, the additional revenue can either be carried forward to the next fiscal year or spent in the current fiscal year.

In either scenario, the actual budget at the end of the fiscal year may be very different from the projected budget at the beginning of the fiscal year. As a result, when viewing an institution's budget, you may see a Projected and an Actual column.

Budgeting Models

While the basic premises described above are standard for all budgets, the process of establishing and adjusting the budget varies from institution to institution. What budget model does your college or university utilize? If you do not know, it is a vital question to ask. Leaders at all levels of higher education must have a keen understanding of the prevailing budget model (e.g., the process for making and adjusting the budget) at the institution where they work, for the budget model provides insight into institutional values. The model utilized will dictate many aspects of your institutional, departmental, and unit goal setting and will dictate what behaviors and organizational actions are rewarded. As stated so eloquently by Jack Lew, 76th Secretary of the Treasury, the budget (and the underlying model that built the budget) is "an expression of our values and aspirations." Not knowing which budget model is utilized at your institution is akin to trying to play a game without understanding the rules.

The most common budget models utilized in higher education are zero-based budgeting, incremental budgeting, formula-based budgeting, and responsibility center management (RCM) (Ruben et al., 2021). The first three models (zero-based, incremental, and formula-based) are considered centralized approaches, while RCM is considered a decentralized approach. Each of these models presents unique opportunities and challenges but all have a profound effect on the way institutions, departments, and units set goals and prioritize actions.

Zero-Based Budgeting

In a zero-based budgeting model, each department's annual budget begins at zero, regardless of what the departmental budget was the previous year. Departments must submit funding requests with justification and decisions are made centrally about how much is allocated to each department. The zero-based budgeting process may help to control costs as departments must justify their budget requests. However, the approach can be time-consuming as institutional leaders must read through departmental justifications and agree on allocations. The process may also be prone to a perceived lack of transparency and political infighting as allocation decisions may be viewed as capricious. Institutions that rely solely on a zero-based budgeting model for resource allocation decisions may value centralized decision-making and accountability. In this type of budgeting environment, departmental leaders must be highly attuned to the strategic goals of college and university leadership and be able to make strong connections between their department's work and the accomplishment of those goals.

Incremental Budgeting

Incremental budgeting is the oldest and most common budgeting approach in higher education (Curry et al., 2013). In this budgeting approach, departments are allocated roughly the same amount they were given the previous year. Depending upon the availability of funding, managers are often tasked with scenario planning for possible across-the-board percentage increases or decreases. The incremental budgeting model is easy to understand, provides stability, allows for planning long-term initiatives, and reduces internal rivalry. However, it does not reward those units that implement cost-saving mechanisms or, through entrepreneurial endeavors, increase revenue dramatically. It may also encourage unnecessary spending as some departments or units may spend all the money allocated each year, whether they need to or not, to obtain a greater amount in the next fiscal year. Lastly, one of the key assumptions of the incremental budgeting model is that revenues and expenses will remain relatively stable. Those who have worked within higher education within the past five years can attest to the fallacy of this assumption, as unforeseen external factors such as the COVID-19 pandemic and widespread inflation wreaked havoc upon enrollment and the cost of operating a higher education institution.

Typically, those institutions that utilize an incremental budgeting model exclusively value simplicity, stability, and internal harmony among units and departments. While entrepreneurial endeavors may be welcome, they may not be greatly rewarded.

Formula-based Budgeting

The formula-based budgeting model (also referred to as performance-based budgeting) allocates funding to departments through a predetermined formula that contains weights for certain outputs such as enrollment numbers, graduation rates, or research volume. This budgeting model has gained popularity in recent decades as accreditors, states, and local municipalities have called for greater accountability from higher education institutions. The formula-based budgeting model provides internal transparency surrounding institutional goals and rewards those units and departments that contribute significantly to meeting those goals. It also provides for transparency to outside stakeholders such as accreditors, taxpayers, legislators, and local council persons with regards to what is being accomplished with tuition dollars and public funding. For example, many institutions may reward departments with whose student retention and graduation rates increase or are above the college/university average with additional funding.

However, such models may not account adequately for funding new initiatives that have not yet had an opportunity to contribute significantly to outcomes. Formula-based budgeting models are also difficult to devise as colleges and universities are complex organizations where tasks are not routine, and it is often difficult to decipher which individual or unit is responsible for any single outcome. Institutions that exclusively utilize a formula-based budgeting model may highly value accountability and transparency with regards to resource allocation. In this type of environment, resources are expected to be aligned strongly with specific institutional goals. When proposing new initiatives or advocating for more resources, a strong case for how such initiatives or additional resources relate to specific institutional outcomes will be warranted.

Responsibility Center Management

RCM is also referred to as revenue-centered budgeting. In an RCM environment, each unit is financially responsible for its own direct and indirect expenditures. In other words, each unit operates, for the most part, like its own business enterprise and must generate enough revenue to cover its own expenses. Indirect costs, such as electricity and information technology support, are estimated for each unit by institutional leaders and charged to the units, respectively. RCM models incentivize entrepreneurship and may lead to a diversification of revenue streams as each unit works independently to identify and capitalize upon revenue opportunities. This diversification of revenue may, in the long term, lead to greater financial security for the institution, broadly. Alternatively, an RCM model may create disincentives for focusing upon less lucrative, yet important, endeavors. In a five-year review of Rutgers University's RCM model, one administrator stated, "it appears to discourage desired behaviors or impede mission-critical programs and initiatives, including those that relate to Ph.D. education, arts, and humanities, diversity, equity, and inclusion, and those that support students or further the university's public mission" (Rutgers University, 2021). RCM may also create barriers to interdisciplinary and interdepartmental collaboration with regards to shared programs and services. Leaders at institutions that utilize an RCM-based budget model must have a strong understanding of revenue generation strategies and expenditure containment. When proposing new initiatives or advocating for more resources, a strong business argument will need to be made with net revenue projections.

Hybrid Approaches

While the four models described above have been presented as distinct and exclusive approaches, most colleges and universities employ more than one model (Carey, 2022). Regardless of which model or hybrid of models is used at a particular institution, leaders at all levels benefit from understanding how resource allocations are made, and the institutional values signaled by that process.

Budget Development: Connecting Institutional Goals to the Departmental Level

Now having a better understanding of the various budgeting models used in higher education, leaders need to understand how to communicate their budget needs in alignment with the institutional strategic plan. The strategic plan offers a glimpse into, "what an organization is, what it does, and why it does it" (Bryson, 2011, p. 26). Therefore, it shouldn't surprise you that decision-makers prioritize allocations that support strategic planning. The more effectively leaders can communicate their alignment with institutional goals, the greater the likelihood of securing financial support.

A leader should be able to ascertain what role their individual department or unit is or should be playing in the overall achievement of institutional goals. A visit to the institutional research or institutional effectiveness office may also prove to be useful. Such offices are usually tasked with measuring progress toward strategic plan goals and documenting each department's contributions in the achievement of the goals. As discussed in Chapter 2, the data that is collected, analyzed, and disseminated becomes a powerful tool in storytelling and engaging decision-makers for buy-in.

Understanding institutional priorities can also aid leaders in advocating for additional resources, when such resources are needed to meet goals. For example, knowing that your institution operates on a zero-based budgeting model, it is imperative that leaders ensure that all funds are spent from the prior year before requesting additional funds in the upcoming year.

Practical Tools and Strategies

To effectively navigate and implement the budgeting models discussed, leaders can utilize a range of practical tools and strategies to better align resources with institutional, departmental, and unit goals, while also advocating for additional resources when necessary.

Learn to Speak as a Budget Expert

Most university staff involved in budget processes are familiar with and utilize the NACUBO standards for classifying and tracking expenditures. Thus, leaders should familiarize themselves with these standards. Doing so will help with understanding how certain expenditures are accounted for within the larger institutional budget.

Ask Key Questions

Leaders should not be shy about getting to know their institution's budgeting process. It will pay long-term dividends. When initially meeting with business administrators, leaders should be sure to ask the following questions:

1. What type of budgeting model(s) do we utilize (zero-based, incremental, formula-based, RCM, or a hybrid approach)?
2. What is the general timeline for developing the budget annually?
3. What has been my department's/unit's annual budget for the past five years (projected and actual)?
4. What percentage of restricted and unrestricted funds does my department/unit receive annually, on average?
5. Of the unrestricted funds, what parameters are put on them?
6. What have been my unit's/department's annual expenditures by NACUBO classification (or any other classification system utilized) for the past five years?
7. How are budget increases requested and what kind of rationale/support is needed?

Evaluate and Build Your Budget

Asking the following questions should provide insightful information on how your department approaches their budget:

1. What were the allocations and expenses in the past five years?
2. What are the anticipated projections for next fiscal year?
3. Are there initiatives underway that are currently not reflected?
4. Are there expenses that no longer require support at their current funding levels that could be reduced (or repurposed to support other areas of the budget)?

Advocating for Additional Resources

When advocating for additional financial resources, leaders must clearly:

1. Identify the institution's major goals as outlined in the strategic plan.
2. Align departmental goals with institutional objectives.
3. Demonstrate how their unit contributes to the student enrollment cycle, including recruitment, retention, and completion.
4. Showcase departmental success on key performance indicators, as underperforming units are less likely to receive additional resources.
5. Articulate the return on investment (ROI), outlining the expected outcomes if additional resources are granted.

A Personal Anecdote

At one point in my career, I was responsible for managing a call center for a large community college. The call center fielded phone calls, emails, and web-based chats from students seeking information about everything from admissions to financial aid to scheduling. When the call center first opened, I knew it was important to track the number of inquiries coming into the call center, the time it took for my employees to respond to such inquiries, and students' satisfaction with the service they received. I therefore advocated for the purchase of a customer relationship management (CRM) platform that would allow me to track these data points. Within a few weeks of data collection it became apparent we did not have enough employees for the volume of inquiries the call center was receiving. Additionally, customer satisfaction data from the surveys that students received following their interaction with a call center employee showed that students were not pleased with the wait times. I even followed up with a few of the unsatisfied students to determine how their wait times influenced their enrollment decisions. For some of them, the wait times had resulted in them either not enrolling or not registering for an additional class. This meant loss of revenue for the college.

I also knew the college operated on an incremental budgeting model and that midyear budget adjustments would be occurring in a few months. I acted quickly to ensure my requests were included in any midyear budget adjustment discussions. When meeting with the college president and chief financial officer, I used data to show how the call center was not adequately staffed, how students felt about the wait times to speak with an employee, how the wait times to speak with an employee had affected the enrollment of some students (and thus the overall enrollment goals of the college), and how many additional staff members I would need to meet demand. The funding for the two additional employees I requested was approved, allowing us to meet demand more effectively. As a result, student satisfaction survey ratings significantly increased. Having the data to demonstrate a need, tying that need to the college's enrollment goal, having a specific request (two additional employees), and knowing where the college was within the budget cycle helped me to successfully advocate for additional resources.

Conclusion

This chapter assisted leaders in defining various budgetary terms (e.g. revenue, expenditures) while introducing various budget models that are often utilized in higher education. Furthermore, it provided a practical framework for leaders in developing a departmental or divisional budget. As discussed in the introduction of this chapter, budgets are crucial for financial planning, strategic planning, and resource allocation. Ultimately, they help institutions align financial resources with their mission and goals.

References

Bryson, J.M. (2011). *Strategic planning for public and nonprofit organizations* (4th edition). Jossey-Bass.

Carey, E. (2022, October). *The big questions: higher education budgeting during and after COVID*. The ACAD Leader. https://acad.org/resource/the-big-questions-higher-education-budgeting-during-and-after-covid/

Curry, J.R., Laws, A.L., & Strauss, J.C. (2013). *Responsibility center management: A guide to balancing academic entrepreneurship with fiscal responsibility.* National Association of College and University Business Officers.

McGee, J. (2016). *Breakpoint: The changing marketplace for higher education.* John Hopkins University Press.

National Center for Education Statistics (2023). Postsecondary Institution Expenses. *Condition of Education.* U.S. Department of Education, Institute of Education Sciences. Retrieved July 26, 2024, from https://nces.ed.gov/programs/coe/indicator/cue

Nietzel, M.T. & Ambrose, C.M. (2024, February 5). Colleges on the brink: broken budgets, not hostile takeovers, are the biggest challenge for most presidents. *Inside Higher Education.* www.insidehighered.com/opinion/views/2024/02/05/most-colleges-finances-are-biggest-challenge-opinion

Ruben, B.D., De Lisi, R., & Gigliotti, R.A. (2021). *A guide for leaders in higher education: concepts, competencies, and tools* (2nd ed.). Stylus.

Rutgers University (2021, June). *RCM at Rutgers: A five-year review.* Retrieved September 20, 2024, from www.rutgers.edu/sites/default/files/2021-08/RCMReviewReport-6-10-21_Final.pdf

Appendix

Sample Departmental Expenditure Categories

Apparel
Advertising
Association Dues
Catering and Food Services
Contractual Services
Equipment
Events and Programming Supplies
Incidentals
Labor
Office Supplies
Postage and Postal Charges
Professional Development
Registration Fees
Telecommunications
Travel

4

Creating and Implementing a Strategic Plan

Mike Hoffshire

INTRODUCTION

Imagine a new vice president is scheduling meetings with department leaders to gain a deeper understanding of the areas they oversee. They've requested an overview of your department's direction, current priorities, and both short-term and long-term goals. In one scenario, despite seeing yourself as a prepared leader, you find yourself scrambling to gather data, solicit input from your team and stakeholders, and must quickly put together a document for the meeting. In another scenario, you are at ease, confidently presenting a comprehensive document that outlines your department's mission, performance metrics, and current goals. You're also able to articulate a clear vision for positioning the unit for success over the next three years and how your goals align with the institution's overarching priorities. Which scenario would you prefer? This is the importance of strategic planning.

Strategic planning helps leaders prepare and respond to the changing environment in which it is situated. If approached

DOI: 10.4324/9781003533856-4

intentionally, strategic planning is a powerful tool that allows individuals, departments, and institutions to gather feedback, set measurable objectives, and think beyond day-to-day work responsibilities. It provides a framework to organize and articulate the steps needed to put together actionable, both short and long term, plans for the organization.

As a leader, it is essential to have a strong understanding of the current state of the areas you oversee. Equally important is the ability to anticipate changes in the surrounding environment. This includes recognizing emerging trends such as increased competition, new state or federal policies, or potential staffing reductions. Hunt et al. (1997) stated that, "Higher education leaders cannot control the future, but they should attempt to identify and isolate present actions and to forecast how results from actions taken now can be expected to influence the future" (p. 14). If approached intentionally and through a relationship-orientated process, strategic planning can be an effective means of promoting operational efficiency.

Failure to utilize a strategic plan can lead to a range of unfavorable outcomes. First, an organization may lack a sense of purpose or direction, which may lead to confusion in priorities. Second, the absence of a strategic plan can lead to an inefficient use of resources. Third, there may be difficulty measuring success—particularly as it relates to benchmarks and key performance indicators. Leaders may not know if the organization is moving in the right direction. Lastly, failure to implement a strategic plan may lead the organization to struggle to adapt to changing environments. As such, it is critical leaders establish clear metrics and hold others accountable for using the strategic plan to ensure desired outcomes are achieved.

While this chapter serves as a strong introduction to strategic planning, readers are encouraged to consult additional resources, such as *How Colleges Change: Understanding, Leading, and Enacting Change* by Adrianna Kezar (2018) and *Strategy Planning for University Colleges and Departments: A Step by Step Guide to Developing, Refining, and Implementing Effective Strategy* by Jayme Renfro (2025). You'll want to immerse yourself in the literature as well as possess an understanding of tools to assist you in the strategic planning process. It is important to note that your institution may have established plans, guidelines, and documents that are accessible, and in some circumstances, required to be followed.

Components of a Strategic Plan

While the process and final outcome of a strategic planning process may differ based on approach, all strategic plans should answer the following questions:

- Who are we? What is the mission of the department?
- What do we do?
- How does our work connect to the institutional mission?
- What is currently happening in the landscape that informs/impacts our work?
- What goals, strategies, and action plans will help us achieve our goals?
- What resources are available to assist us?
- What is the timeline for completion?
- Who is accountable?

A sample table of contents of a strategic plan can be found in the Appendix.

Guiding Principles for Strategic Planning

While there is no one-size-fits-all approach, the following should serve as guiding principles for leaders to consider when developing the strategic planning process they intend to utilize. These principles below are not intended to be utilized in a linear fashion as leadership styles and institutional context may influence how the process is developed. Regardless of the approach chosen, it will be your responsibility to guide the process, encourage participation, and ensure inclusivity among all constituents. Later, you'll advocate for plan integration and execution (as well as hold your team accountable).

Planning to Plan

A critical component of the strategic planning process involves an appropriate planning period. In this stage, leaders should decide on the process to utilize, who will be involved, and the timeline. Additionally, leaders should leverage insight gathered from their institution, department, budget, and data (Chapters 1–3) to inform the direction of their strategic plan. Examples include a review of the mission and values, organization chart(s), performance data, key performance metrics, and financial documents. Subsequently, these documents become the foundation to inform the first pages of your written strategic plan. It will help to inform your strategies and goals of your unit or division that ultimately should be in alignment with the overall mission and vision of the institution.

It is also imperative for you to develop a timeline with established deadlines for key milestones (e.g., town halls and forums, drafts of a written strategic plan, due dates). This ensures accountability amongst yourself and your stakeholders in the strategic planning process in the midst of day-to-day operations and responsibilities. At a minimum, the strategic planning process should take approximately six months. Refer to your departmental, divisional- and institutional-wide calendars to ensure the timeline does not conflict or overlap with major events.

Team Engagement

It is important to introduce your team to the concept of strategic planning. This not only provides you with an opportunity to define strategic planning, but gain buy-in for those that directly report to you. Questions to help guide the conversation with your team could include:

- What is a strategic plan?
- What is the purpose of a strategic plan?
- Why are we conducting a strategic plan?
- What are some of the potential outcomes of a strategic plan?

The answers to these questions allow you to engage in a meaningful conversation with your team. However, the strategic planning process is sometimes met with pushback as individuals fear the unknown, including potential outcomes, such as elimination of services or re-organizations. Others may feel anxiety over written goals and action items. As the leader, it is important you consider concerns raised openly and thoughtfully. Promoting a culture of transparency and creativity is imperative to gaining trust in this process.

Constituent Engagement
In addition to engaging your team, it is important to consider what stakeholders you'll engage as you undertake this process. Often, these stakeholders are closely intertwined with your work and can provide valuable insight into the current state of the organization, as well as future opportunities. As a leader, you may request feedback from survey instruments, focus groups, and town halls. Questions to help guide your conversations with stakeholders could include:

- What are the strengths of our organization?
- What do we do well? What needs improvement?
- What is currently happening in the landscape that threatens our success?

Participation from team members and stakeholders leads to a number of positive outcomes. First, participation enhances diverse perspectives and provides valuable insights from different levels of the organization. Second, individuals may feel a renewed sense of engagement within the organization, as they may have the opportunity to lead various aspects of the strategic planning process. This may reduce potential resistance later on in the implementation phase. Third, it allows for personal and professional competency development. By gaining a better understanding of the strategic planning process, individuals learn what strategy is, how to create it, and what it means for the organization.

Goal Creation

Using the feedback generated from constituents, in concert with the documents collected, goals and strategies can be developed after a careful analysis of the data and consolidated into larger themes. Successful strategic planning documents typically contain four to six goals with approximately a dozen initiatives (Hanover Research, 2013). The following questions should guide leaders in plan creation:

- What do we do very well?
- What are our opportunities for improvement?
- What are we (team, department, division, organization) being asked to do?
- How can we accomplish those tasks?
- What is currently happening in the landscape that threatens our success?
- What are new programs and/or services we could offer?
- What are existing programs and/or services we want to (or are being required to) enhance?
- What are existing programs and/or services we want to discontinue?
- What is our timeline for doing this?

For example, as a department supervisor overseeing career services, your department is responsible for matching students with job opportunities/employers after graduation. National trends indicate that competition for jobs is increasing with students requiring additional skill sets for success. Additional feedback from the team has illuminated a student's interest in meeting with more employers throughout the academic year. With decreased institutional support for travel and funding for employer engagement, you are evaluating ways to provide additional opportunities to create platforms for employers and students to connect and network. In review of the institutional strategic plan there is support for strategies that embrace technological literacy. At the intersection of these elements, a theme has emerged for using technology (as a time-saving and fiscally efficient strategy) to enhance the breadth and depth of employer to student engagement. As such, a goal can be established and developed to secure resources (e.g., technological platforms) that creates more opportunities for networking and interviewing.

Measurements and Tracking

For each goal and strategy addressed in the strategic plan, there should be a way to measure or assess its progress or success. For example, the Director of Student Involvement may have a goal of increasing student participation in student organizations within a three-year timeframe. Metrics such as the number of students who become members of student organizations throughout each year or the number of events held each semester can help track progress. Having strong measurements allows leaders to assess effectiveness, identify areas for improvement, and document progress. Furthermore, it may lead to a change in strategy with obtaining a particular goal of the strategic plan.

Accountability

While ensuring each goal of the strategic plan has a measurement, it is equally important to assign key individuals or departments responsible for its implementation. Therefore, leaders are able to provide guidance on the particular goal and strategy while knowing who is responsible for its success. Typically, the individuals and offices are closely related in title (or function) to the goal outlined. As a best practice, leaders should check in frequently. Finally, assigning individuals or offices allows for continuity of strategy in the event of staff turnover. As a leader, it is your responsibility to ensure a successful implementation of the strategic plan.

Consider Financial Costs

When implementing a strategic plan, it is important to consider the financial costs. As a leader, you will need to determine the resources required to execute each goal outlined in the strategic plan. Examples may include marketing, operations, or research and development. If the strategic plan requires new skills or knowledge, employees may need to be trained. You should also consider new technology to aid in the monitoring and progress of various aspects of the plan. While it may be feasible to monitor goals at the departmental or divisional level, software (e.g., Envisio) may be needed at the institutional level. Lastly, a key consideration may be asking yourself and supervisor(s) what support may be available for such a project. In addition to established written resources, you may ask for additional staffing, interns, student support, funding, etc. In some instances, it may be beneficial to bring in consultants to drive this process.

Documentation
Consideration must be given to how the strategic plan and the final outcome will be presented. Most institutions, departments, and divisions choose to write a formal, written report but recently, the use of multimedia (e.g., videos, audio, slideshows) are becoming more prevalent. It can also be tailored to a specific audience. For your team, you might organize a half-day retreat where use of an extensive document may be utilized. For your supervisor or vice president, you could provide a shorter document that highlights the goals and strategies of the unit. Perhaps for a meeting with a task force or committee, you will have a concise PowerPoint of the plan that guides these constituents through the main points.

Monitoring and Evaluation
It is common for higher education leaders to believe that the strategic planning process concludes once the document is completed. It is easy to place the completed document on a shelf to collect dust, only for it to be revisited once or twice a year. However, best practices suggest that consistent engagement, along with thorough monitoring and evaluating, is critical.

These check-in opportunities allow for open discussion about progress on each goal, being transparent about setbacks, identifying areas that may need more attention, and documenting plan adjustments. While monitoring progress, leaders must remain flexible in their approach to strategic planning goals and strategies, adapting as needed in response to changing conditions.

Examples include new administrative leadership, resource allocation, or market competition. Under these circumstances, a change to specific measures or evaluation may be necessary.

Benefits and Challenges of Strategic Planning

Without a doubt, the strategic planning process can assist a department, division, or institution in coping with an uncertain future. It helps to situate the organization within its current environment and to provide unity in mission, programs, and values. An established strategic plan should acknowledge and promote institutional activities with environmental demands.

Additionally, by making clear connections between departmental, divisional, and institutional goals, leaders can align institutional goals and objectives to one another, reduce redundancies in workflows and promote a seamless learning environment for students. The benefits of a strategic plan include allowing leaders to advocate for higher budgets or more resources through the use of the strategic plan. For example, a strategic plan for a tutoring center may include the establishment of an online tutoring platform. Despite the students' demand for expanded hours and options beyond in-person tutoring, administration fails to support such an initiative. However, after reviewing the campus-wide strategic plan, you find an objective that states, "Provide students with increased access to support and resources 24/7." By making connections for how your needs (online tutoring) align with institutional values and strategies (24/7 support and resources), you were successful in receiving future funding.

This chapter would be remiss not to discuss some of the challenges associated with strategic planning in higher education settings. First, strategic planning is a complex and intricate process that does not provide for an immediate, prescriptive formula for organizational success. As such, strategic planning must have a strong commitment from leadership. Individuals must believe that their involvement matters and that they will benefit from engaging in the process. Otherwise, it is simply viewed as another top-down approach to enacting change. Second, one of the most common reasons for strategic planning failure is a lack of ownership and follow-through. As a leader, we encourage you to set clear objectives and assign individuals responsible for implementation. As discussed, communicate with your constituents often and check in regarding progress on each goal or initiative outlined in your plan. This can be done individually or in group meetings. Third, strategic planning may actually stifle or inhibit immediate changes that could greatly benefit the organization. It assumes the organization operates in a static environment and requires extensive planning, significant stakeholder engagement, and comprehensive documentation. As such, consider the use of adaptive models of strategic planning, which are more flexible, risk-aware and data driven. This type of planning allows ongoing planning in dynamic and flexible environments.

Conclusion

In conclusion, strategic planning is the process by which an institution can develop a shared vision of its future using intentional and measurable steps to get there. Most higher education organizations tend to develop five-to-ten-year strategic plans at a university level.

However, at the departmental level, an annual (or bi-annual) plan may be more appropriate to align with fiscal planning practices. Regardless of length, the document should clearly articulate the organization's plan and serve to inform, influence, anchor, and guide the organization's future.

This chapter has reviewed the multiple steps a leader should consider when undertaking such a process. Whether conducted at the institutional, divisional, or departmental level, strategic planning can assist leaders in providing guidance on making decisions, both long term and day to day. Ultimately, strategic planning provides opportunities for leadership and employees to join together to dream big and enact intentional change within their organizations.

References

Hanover Research. (2013). Strategic planning in higher education: Best practices and benchmarking. www.hanoverresearch.com/insights-blog/higher-education/strategic-planning-in-higher-education-best-practices-and-benchmarking

Hunt, C. M., Oosting, K. W., Stevens, R., Loudon, D., & Migliore, R. H. (1997). *Strategic planning for higher education*. Haworth Press. https://api.pageplace.de/preview/DT0400.9781135024345_A24419454/preview-9781135024345_A24419454.pdf

Kezar, K. (2018). *How colleges change: Understanding, leading, and enacting change*. Routledge.

Renfro, J. (2025). *Strategic planning for university colleges and departments: A step by step guide to developing, refining, and implementing effective strategy*. Routledge.

Appendix

Sample Table of Contents for Departmental Strategic Plan

To visualize the final output of a strategic plan, please reference a sample table of contents:

I. Executive Summary
    A. Purpose of the Plan
    B. Relevant Data
    C. Summary of Strategic Priorities
    D. Key Goals and Metrics

II. Department Overview
    A. Institutional Strategic Plan
    B. Mission and Vision
    C. Organizational Structure
    D. Key Programs and Services

III. Overview of the Landscape/Landscape Analysis
    A. Internal Strengths and Challenges
    B. External Opportunities and Threats
    C. Peer Institutional Analysis
    D. Economic, Demographic, Financial, Legal, Political Trends
    E. Stakeholder Summary

IV. Strategic Priorities & Action Plans (Where Are We Going/How Will)
V. Key Performance Indicators
VI. Resources
VII. Appendices

5

Knowing the Rules to Be Good at the Game: Understanding University Policy and Procedure

Sonia Valencia

INTRODUCTION

My higher education experience has centered with federal TRIO programs. On my first day of work, after completing new employee orientation, my supervisor provided me with a copy of our grant and the management requirements. These guidance documents included the federal policies that govern TRIO programs and services, objectives, and allowable expenses. I recall being overwhelmed by everything I had read and wondered how I would be expected to remember everything. At the end of my first week I asked my supervisor, "What happens if I forget one of the regulations and do something deemed unallowable?" He jokingly said, "Well, you would be breaking the law and would have to face the consequences." I recognized in his chiding tone a bit of teasing from one seasoned professional to a newbie, but there was a kernel of truth in what he said and I feared making a mistake that could cost me my job or jeopardize the integrity of the grant.

I am now entering nine years as a TRIO professional, and my relationship with regulations, policies, and procedures has significantly shifted; I no longer fear them or see them as obstacles, but rather as a reference for what leaders should be doing (and how they do it). As I have advanced in my career and stepped into a director role, I am responsible for being familiar with regulations, policies, and procedures at the federal, state, and divisional levels to guide my team. My goal is to demonstrate why and how it is beneficial that higher education professionals understand the intimate interplay between policies and regulations. It is within this context that managers who possess a deep understanding of policies and regulations can drive organizational efficiency and ensure student services are aligned with institutional goals. I welcome the chance to help new professionals see these directives not as challenges or barriers, but as guides.

Federal Policies and Higher Education

Macro-level policies, including federal laws such as the Family Educational Rights and Privacy Act (FERPA), Title IX, and the Americans with Disabilities Act (ADA), provide regulations that protect students' rights and promulgate equity. They also shape higher education's micro-level operations. As such, division and departmental leaders should comply with these policies and ensure they, and their teams, are familiar with them. Oftentimes, compliance is achieved through training, policy and procedure handbooks, and certifications, which are common methods for ensuring departmental regulatory compliance.

While familiarity and training of federal policies is a critical step, it is equally important to establish processes for ongoing monitoring of shifts in policy changes. Managers must be prepared to conduct frequent policy audits to ensure compliance. Achieving operational efficiency requires a skill to promptly understand, interpret, and respond adequately to evolving changes in federal policies. For example, for many years, participation in federal TRIO programs was limited to students who were U.S. citizens or permanent residents. However, in 2022, under the Performance Partnership Pilot ("P3") for Disconnected Youth, the Department of Education waived the immigration status requirements in California and Oregon. Traditionally, this requirement was perceived as a significant barrier for a particular group of students. These changes, although on a federal level, directly impacted and informed our approaches to our daily work. Our team reviewed the P3 statement and discussed the changes our office needed to adopt to ensure compliance. This included a comprehensive review of the recruitment, application, and selection process to identify changes. As a result, we updated our website and marketing materials, performed a comprehensive review of our application and strategized new recruitment strategies for undocumented students. Ideally, these yearly reviews will encourage meaningful conversations, resulting in revised procedures that foster efficiency, equity and compliance.

Table 5.1 provides some key federal policies that significantly impact higher education in the United States. It is essential for leaders to familiarize themselves so they ensure effective governance and avoid potential legal challenges.

TABLE 5.1 Federal Policies in Higher Education

Policy	Description/Key Notes
Higher Education Act (HEA)	Governs federal financial aid programs like Pell Grants and Work-Study.
Title IX	Prohibits sex-based discrimination in federally funded education programs.
Americans with Disabilities Act (ADA)	Protects students and employees with disabilities, requiring reasonable accommodations.
Family Educational Rights and Privacy Act (FERPA)	Ensures the privacy of student educational records and governs their disclosure.
The Jeanne Clery Disclosure of Campus Security Policy and Campus Crime Statistics Act (Clery Act)	Requires institutions to disclose campus crime statistics, safety policies, and procedures for handling crime reports to ensure transparency and campus safety.

As demonstrated through the P3 pilot example, laws change and evolve at the federal level and guide our responses in our daily work. This section outlined several federal policies to undertake an initial review within your department. Chapters 6 and 9 will further explore these concepts.

Statewide Policies

While federal policies provide overarching frameworks that reflect national commitments, state laws are attuned to local needs or where federal law does not have purview. State laws can also mandate that institutions comply with requirements beyond federal law (provided they do not conflict). Examples in higher education include admissions (admissions requirements), student support (diversity, equity, and inclusion) and campus safety (open carry). In the state of California, for instance, financial aid has expanded to include additional funding for need-based aid. Known as the "Cal Grant," it provides for financial assistance in the form of a one time award to offset attendance at a California higher education institution. Eligibility is based on students' FAFSA or CA Dream Act application responses, verified grade point average, and the type of California intended college. This funding makes higher education more accessible to students with financial need attending public institutions. This grant funding, which works in tandem with Title IV of the Higher Education Act, reflects state interests and commitments to addressing gaps in financial need.

There are several key reasons why leaders in higher education must stay informed about statewide policies. More importantly, there are significant consequences if they fail to effectively engage with these policies. Ensuring adherence to governing laws and policies is crucial to maintaining the integrity of our work, a responsibility shared by all professionals in fields influenced by federal or state regulations. Statewide policies may be felt more directly than federal ones, particularly when it comes to

TABLE 5.2 State Policies in Higher Education

Policy	Description	Examples
State Financial Aid Policies	Addresses state-specific financial aid needs.	Cal Grant (California), TEXAS Grant (Texas), Taylor Opportunity Program for Students
State Education Budget Allocations (Public institutions)	Directly impacts tuition, fees, and institutional priorities.	University System of Georgia – Board of Regents, Utah Board of Higher Education
Free Tuition Programs/State Promise Programs	Helps reduce the overall debt students pursuing a college education at an institution.	University of Texas Systems Promise Plus Program (2022). Other states that have similar promises include Georgia and Ohio.
Tuition Regulation Policies	Establishes a funding baseline for K-14 institutions.	California's Prop 98 (1988)
Statewide Workforce Development Policies	Workforce development policies funnel state and federal funds to expand career training programs and strengthen higher education and industry partnerships, reflecting the state's economic priorities.	Massachusetts Workforce Skills Cabinet, Ohio's TechCred Program, Maryland's EARN Program (Employment Advancement Right Now)

budget allocations for education. As residents of a particular state, higher education professionals possess unique insights into the needs of both students and institutions, positioning them to advocate for and help shape policies that will influence their work and the students they serve.

Statewide policies are crucial in higher education for many reasons, including alignment with state priorities, equity and access, accountability, resource allocation, and economic growth. Table 5.2 provides examples of common statewide policies that may impact leaders' work.

Unpacking Institutional Policies and Procedures

If federal and state policies contour the landscape of higher education, institutional and divisional policies chisel out the details that guide daily operations. There is an element of constancy to federal and statewide policies as they appear no matter where you live within the country or state. While it is important to keep federal and state policies in your purview, keep in mind there are institutional leaders (president, provost, vice presidents, deans, etc.) that are responsible for executing changes within the organization to develop an institutional response. The changes within the organization are to ensure compliance and generate guidelines for managers to adapt and align their practices. The guidelines developed from institutional leaders are then operationalized through institutional policies and procedures.

As the name suggests, institutional and divisional policies and procedures change from institution to institution and can vary significantly within the same institution. Thus, leaders must be familiar with institutional policies that shape what their department does (and how it operates to complete tasks). Table 5.3 provides examples of institutional policies that are often found within higher education organizations.

As a starting point for learning and utilizing institutional policy manuals, this chapter will focus on those policies found in

TABLE 5.3 Institutional Policy Examples

Academic Catalog	Acts as a contract detailing academic requirements, courses, and program structures.
Employee Handbook	Covers workplace expectations, benefits, leave policies, and conflict resolution.
Travel Policy	Defines procedures for planning, approval, and reimbursement for travel expenses.
Purchasing Policy	Outlines procurement processes, required approvals, and use of procurement cards.
Performance Evaluations	Details processes for staff reviews, including merit-based decisions and dispute resolution.
Events Planning	Policies governing campus events, including space reservations and risk management.
Risk Management	Ensures compliance with safety and liability standards for campus and off-campus activities.

the academic catalog, employee handbook, and purchasing and travel regulation.

Academic Catalog and (Under)Graduate Policies

An institution's academic catalog contains critical policies and procedures that govern students' academic journeys. As the catalog contains university, college, and major requirements by year, we can think of the catalog as a contract between students and the institution. Consequently, student-facing areas, including advising, financial aid, or the registrar, must be well versed in the policies and procedures outlined in the academic catalog to ensure students receive accurate advising and support to persist. To this end, understanding what constitutes good academic standing or outlining the criteria for academic probation is essential. Additionally, the student code of conduct is a critical set of policies involving academic integrity and responsible behavior, amongst other topics, of which the university community upholds.

Employee Handbook

The employee handbook is a comprehensive guide that covers expectations and policies that impact all employees. All faculty, staff, interns, and student workers should be intimately familiar with it on day one. The handbook presents information about benefits, leave policies, performance management, compensation, and dress code expectations. It is in an employee's interest to know the rights and privileges the institution affords them. Consequently, people with supervisory responsibilities should be familiar with key policies that will help ensure workplace equity and institutional compliance. Policies governing equal employment opportunity (EEO), time and leave as well as grievance procedures can often be found in the employee handbook.

EEO (including reasonable accommodation and accessibility) policies help ensure an equitable workplace. EEO policies might include information about hiring and employee evaluation processes that supervisors must implement. Supervisors want to help their teams receive any accommodations or support they may need to grow, thrive, and execute their roles. As such, supervisors should know how to respond and where to refer employees needing additional accommodations.

Within employee handbooks, leaders will find definitions and processes for utilizing sick and vacation leave for both themselves and their staff. Often, a supervisor's duties include reviewing and approving timesheets and leave requests. In my career, I have worked at institutions where documentation accompanying sick leave must be turned into human resources. Others may allow for a more flexible arrangement, allowing two or three days to submit documentation. Knowledge of the institution's approach to adjacent policies such as the Family and Medical Leave Act (FMLA) is also essential for supervisors. Upholding labor laws and handling time off requests equitably are key supervisor expectations guided by policies that govern these areas.

The employee handbook will also provide for the process of handling grievances and/or conflict within the organization. Supervisors should be well versed in what procedures and resources are available to assist in resolving disagreements. Similarly, supervisors should inform their team about the institution's staff complaint and grievance processes. Conflict is inevitable, and navigating it can engender many different feelings, but understanding the institution's process for handling conflict can help supervisors feel confident engaging in conflict resolution or addressing grievances.

Purchasing and Travel

Navigating purchasing and travel in a way that upholds institutional policies and expectations is critical to ensuring that departments can acquire the goods they need to conduct university business without any delays. Depending on a department's policies, purchasing might require different levels of approval.

Therefore, knowing and understanding the levels of approval as well as respective timeframes required can ensure that goods and services are received in a timely fashion. For example, an institution's purchasing process may require that all requisition requests include a rationale and quote for approval by their supervisor.

Throughout my employment trajectory in higher education, I have experienced vast differences in student and staff travel processes. What has remained constant throughout, however, is the necessity for me to stay abreast of changes. For example, after organizing and participating in staff-led travel for years at an institution, I was surprised when my request was denied because I needed an active driving safety certificate on file. A driving safety certification had not previously been required, so I was surprised and caught off guard when I learned it was required 24 hours before our scheduled departure. In this situation, not staying abreast of changes to travel policy resulted in lost funds, as the conference registrations and hotel deposits associated with the conference were not refunded.

The institutional resources outlined above serve as an essential guide for leaders from day one. These resources emphasize the importance of taking responsibility—whether it's for managing university funds, overseeing employees, or ensuring positive workplace conditions. Leaders must remember that asking for forgiveness is not an option; these responsibilities are fundamental.

Practical Applications and Recommendations

As a professional whose academic and professional journey has traversed many state lines, I have found that onboarding processes, that include links to relevant policies and procedures, have made familiarizing myself with the university infinitely easier. This chapter provided an overview of federal, state, and institutional policies leaders should collect and comprehend. The Appendix presents a complete chart in which you can begin to examine and unpack key policies and procedures as a manager. When provided with these policies in advance, I have felt better equipped to hit the ground running—whether reserving event rooms, organizing student travel, or approving staff time off requests and timesheets. I have realized that having key policies localized into one single document is incredibly helpful for all professionals. Once collected, here are four recommendations on proceeding:

- **Apply to Daily Operations**: Use the table given in the Appendix to train new employees during onboarding. Share the table with staff to ensure team-wide alignment with policies.
- **Cross-Check for Compliance**: Verify that workflows and departmental practices align with the policies listed. Update your team's procedures as needed to reflect these policies.
- **Monitor Policy Changes**: Assign a team member to monitor federal, state, and institutional policy updates. Add new policies or update descriptions as needed.
- **Create a Feedback Loop**: Create a process for team members to suggest edits or additions, such as a shared comment form or email thread. Encourage your team to document recommendation changes throughout the year.

As I have advanced into a leadership role, I make it a point to use these three levels of governing policies to guide our internal policy and procedure manual for the department. Furthermore, it's important to continue monitoring external and institutional policies and interpret their meaning in the context of our roles and offices.

Conclusion and Implications for Day-to-Day Operations

Institutional, divisional, and departmental policies and procedures must coexist in a harmonious and symbiotic relationship. Federal and statewide policies are slower to change than institutional and divisional policies, as the former requires legislative discussions, reviews, and agreements within a specific/designated legislative session. Departmental procedures are impacted by, and should be in lockstep with, external policies and procedures. As such, institutional policies ought to operate within the institutional and divisional frameworks provided to ensure all workflows move without issues.

Proceed to the next chapter for a detailed policy and procedure manual. A detailed departmental policy and procedure manual can set up teams for success and be a helpful aspect of the onboarding process.

Appendix

Key Policies and Procedures

Policy Area	Policy	Description/Key Notes
National Policies	Higher Education Act (HEA)	Governs federal financial aid programs like Pell Grants and Work-Study.
National Policies	Title IX	Prohibits sex-based discrimination in federally funded education programs.
National Policies	Americans with Disabilities Act (ADA)	Protects students and employees with disabilities, requiring reasonable accommodations.
National Policies	Family Educational Rights and Privacy Act (FERPA)	Ensures the privacy of student educational records and governs their disclosure.
National Policies	The Jeanne Clery Disclosure of Campus Security Policy and Campus Crime Statistics Act (Clery Act)	Requires institutions to disclose campus crime statistics, safety policies, and procedures for handling crime reports to ensure transparency and campus safety.
State Policies	State Financial Aid Policies	Examples: Cal Grant (California), TEXAS Grant (Texas), addressing state-specific financial aid needs.
State Policies	State Education Budget Allocations	Directly impacts tuition, fees, and institutional priorities.
Institutional Policies	Academic Catalog	Acts as a contract detailing academic requirements, courses, and program structures.

(continued)

Policy Area	Policy	Description/Key Notes
Institutional Policies	Employee Handbook	Covers workplace expectations, benefits, leave policies, and conflict resolution.
Institutional Policies	Travel Policy	Defines procedures for planning, approval, and reimbursement for travel expenses.
Institutional Policies	Purchasing Policy	Outlines procurement processes, required approvals, and use of procurement cards.
Institutional Policies	Performance Evaluations	Details processes for staff reviews, including merit-based decisions and dispute resolution.
Institutional Policies	Events Planning	Policies governing campus events, including space reservations and risk management.
Institutional Policies	Risk Management	Ensures compliance with safety and liability standards for campus and off-campus activities.
Divisional Policies	Purchasing	Policies tailored to division-specific needs for procurement and spending limits.
Divisional Policies	Travel	Division-specific travel procedures, including additional approval layers.

6

Leadership in Day-to-Day Operations of Higher Education Administration

Melvin (Jai) Jackson and Kevin McClain

INTRODUCTION

While the previous chapter outlined the initial policies to identify at a federal, state, and institutional level, this chapter provides the rationale and steps for creating an internal and departmental-focused Policy and Procedure Manual (PPM). As a reminder, university policies and procedures are tools that establish practices and parameters at an institutional level. The primary purpose of creating an internal operations policy is to clarify the department's functions, roles, and tasks. A secondary goal of developing an internal PPM is to foster office autonomy and efficiency, allowing staff to operate confidently and independently. Directors, assistant vice presidents (AVPs), and vice presidents (VPs) often operate in a complex space of delicately balancing the needs and priorities of university leadership while also providing management and supervision to staff. In summary, administrators must juggle numerous responsibilities, from monitoring budgets, managing staff, and making progress toward institutional strategic planning objectives. A well-developed internal PPM creates a blueprint for operational efficiency daily for teams in an office setting.

To conceptualize the importance of day-to-day operations, imagine the following scenarios and consider how a lack of scenario planning in these circumstances may lead to a lack of efficiency, safety concerns, or clarity. Combined, these circumstances may lead to frustration for staff and managers. Finally, leaders will understand how day-to-day operations contribute to effective leadership in higher education administration.

Case Study 1: Cross-Training and Turnover

The administrative assistant is unexpectedly sick and has been out of the office for two weeks. Suddenly, no one knows how to check the mail, where keys to the storage closet are, or how to handle lost and found. This has created a discontinuity of tasks and inefficiency within the office. With the administrative assistant gone, the meaningful tasks they complete for the office are suddenly not carried over after their absence. You are the director, and suddenly, you are now using time between meetings with staff to try to learn their job. Significant time is spent rediscovering lost institutional knowledge, learning how to complete tasks, determining who should handle them, and creating resources for training and instruction. Having a documented process (or PPM) that outlines essential office operations ensures cross-training and continuity in tasks that affect everyone in the office. Indeed, it is easy to document processes to facilitate cross-training and contingency plans for the expected absences; however, unexpected absences (or staff turnover) impact the efficiency of day-to-day operations. The authors assert that documenting processes and contingency planning are ongoing exercises that managers should consistently engage in and maintain.

Case Study 2: Standards for Customer Service

You are the director of admissions at a local college. The VP of enrollment management calls you into a meeting to discuss recent inquiries that prospective students cannot reach their admissions advisor. The excessive student complaints on customer service have escalated to leadership. You ask for specific examples and discuss the inquiries with your team of admission advisors. The admissions advisors are shocked at the feedback and confirm they did respond to the students. Upon further investigation, you confirm the advisors' response; however, it may be a week or two until emails or voicemails are returned. In this case, an internal procedures manual can be the starting point for a conversation on expectations and customer service. Furthermore, it can be an opportunity to scaffold advisors' schedules in advance, to create "quiet time" or "administrative hours" where staff block off appointments and meetings to respond to student inquiries. Without an internal procedure, staff may not have known the timeline for a response or that the option exists to hold space on the calendar.

Case Study 3: Safety and Risk Management

You are a director of academic advising and receive a call from the Title IX office. The call concerns a student complaint about uncomfortable discussions in a advisor's office that were deemed inappropriate. This meeting occurred outside of established office hours with limited staff and colleagues to witness. In a follow-up meeting with the Title IX Officer, the academic advisor asserts they were made uncomfortable by the conversation. This is not an ideal circumstance and may be unavoidable; however, an internal policy and procedure could have outlined guidelines to create a space that prioritizes safety and fosters transparency. For example, a document could have suggested the parameters for meeting with students behind closed doors while balancing the need for confidential conversations. Perhaps the policy would suggest that closed-door meetings with students not occur after hours or provide guidance on alerting backup staff to remain as a witness during one-on-one meetings.

Case Study 4: Contextualize University Policy

You are a department chair of a program in the college of education. You have a meeting at 12:30 p.m. with the dean and other department chairs to review the tenure review policy. As you leave the office, you realize it is suspiciously quiet, but the phone is ringing, and students are walking in for help. The staff in your office suite have all taken the student workers to lunch to celebrate a birthday. You appreciate and encourage the collegiality and community spirit; however, you must reschedule your 12:30 p.m. meeting with faculty colleagues. Instead of engaging internal stakeholders to review a policy, you must now staff the front desk. Although admirable, and students are the primary purpose for our work, this scenario does not advance director-level goals or support operational efficiency. In this case, a PPM would have outlined the expectations around coverage for the front desk, established backups, and included a protocol for communication if staff must depart from phones and walk-ins.

The case studies above demonstrate how having a PPM is not granular, insignificant, or micromanaging. In each case, a leader was responsible for tasks or deliverables at the director level but struggled to advance departmental goals due to a lack of clear processes (or focus). We will now explicitly outline the benefits of a PPM, identify the steps to creating a manual, and how our values shape and inform supervision, management, and internal policy.

Benefits of a Day-to-Day Operations Manual

As outlined in the prior case studies, the lack of a PPM could result in inefficient use of time, poor customer service, unnecessary and overabundance of uncomfortable conversations, or employee confusion. Additionally, the lack of an operations manual can lead to a potential oversight of daily, weekly, monthly, quarterly, or annual tasks. As such, PPMs have several inherent benefits for staff, leadership, and the broader institution.

For staff within the office, an internal procedures manual can provide clarity of tasks and increase productivity. The first case study addressed cross-training and turnover when staff must cover office tasks. The absence of a guiding document can lead to errors, mistakes, or tasks simply not being completed (which may have later implications that must be resolved). Additionally, the manager may not always be present to answer questions and provide guidance in real time. The need to constantly ask questions to accomplish daily tasks, although collaborative, may not be the best use of time for the manager; it also prevents staff from confidently approaching the work. Instead, internal procedures can empower team members to approach scenarios promptly and confidently. With a document, staff can feel equipped with advanced tools and empowered to approach scenarios confidently. Ultimately, it positions the staff for success and autonomy.

For leaders, streamlined processes reduce the need for constant troubleshooting and crisis management, allowing more time to focus on strategic planning, innovation, and long-term goals. Clear workflow and scheduling measures also enhance efficiency, as leaders can rely on cross-training procedures and scenario planning for office operations to continue autonomously (without consistent leadership intervention). Indeed, staff autonomy with confidence is the hallmark of a well-functioning team. As discussed in Case Study 4, the scenario where all staff went to lunch simultaneously, a pre-established policy on coverage for the front desk also would have created space for the manager to accomplish their daily goals. This efficiency enables leaders to be more proactive rather than reactive, driving progress and development across the institution.

From an organizational perspective, operational efficiency leads to cost savings, improved service delivery, and greater employee and student satisfaction. When daily operations run smoothly, fewer resources are allocated to redundant tasks, and the institution can allocate more time and energy to mission-critical activities such as academic excellence, research, and student support. Efficient operations also foster a positive work environment, reduce frustration among staff and faculty and contribute to higher retention rates. Furthermore, institutions with strong day-to-day operations are better positioned to adapt to changing external pressures, such as new regulations or shifts in student demographics, thereby enhancing overall institutional resilience.

One overarching benefit of an internal procedure manual for staff, leaders, and institutions is the proactive discussions that develop a clear path for accountability. For many leaders, having accountability conversations with direct reports on misconduct, low performance, or staff not meeting expectations can be uncomfortable. With the document as a reference point, there is a clear and objective policy that can be the starting point to guide the following questions:

- What occurred in this scenario?
- What do our internal policies and procedures say about this?
- What did we collectively agree to do when this particular scenario occurred?
- Did those documented next steps occur?

For operational efficiency to be achieved, leaders must set clear expectations for all stakeholders involved in administrative processes, from department heads to support staff. Moreover, accountability should be shared across all levels of the institution. Faculty and staff should be empowered to take ownership of their responsibilities while remaining accountable to their peers and supervisors.

Developing an Operations Manual

Creating an effective operations manual involves a structured and collaborative approach to meet the organization's needs. This is a linear process that clearly articulates six steps to implementation:

- Step 1: Obtain university policy and procedures (previous chapter)

- Step 2: Form the table of contents
- Step 3: Collaboratively initiate the project plan with the team
- Step 4: Present the operations manual
- Step 5: Create a plan for ongoing maintenance, modifications, and recertification

Step 1: Obtain University Policy and Procedures (Chapter 5)

Building an effective day-to-day PPM requires aligning university policy and procedure with those that you plan to implement. To initiate this process, leaders should start by assessing existing workflows and identifying opportunities to streamline processes and improve efficiency (while remaining compliant with university regulations).

In short, managers should first ask the following two questions:

- What are the university policies and procedures that currently exist that inform our work?
- How do we operationalize them within the context and needs of our unit?

Step 2: Form the Table of Contents

The Appendix presents a table of contents for an internal PPM to illustrate the scenario planning managers can anticipate. By reviewing this table, leaders can develop their own day-to-day operations manual. Engaging in these topics early and establishing protocols and engagement within the department can lead to greater operational efficiency in the workplace. To develop a relevant table of contents for your specific unit, we propose the following sample questions:

- What expectations do we want to set for ourselves and the unit?
- What are the processes that guide our work?
- What are the department's office hours?
- What are the expectations for reporting and taking leave?
- What are quarterly, term, and annual deadlines?
- What are the next steps if a student leaves an expensive item in the office?

Step 3: Collaboratively Initiate Project Plan with Team

Effective day-to-day operations in higher education require input from multiple stakeholders to ensure that the administrative framework aligns with the institution's goals and diverse needs. Administrative leaders, faculty, and support staff should be involved in decision-making. This collaborative approach fosters a sense of ownership, increasing team members' commitment to these values. Team members bring unique perspectives and contribute firsthand insights into operational challenges and needs. Involving these groups ensures that operational decisions reflect the realities of those working within the system, fostering a sense of shared responsibility and ownership.

Reaching consensus on operational processes and shared values requires collaboration and open dialogue. This inclusive approach ensures that operational decisions are not top-down, but instead reflect the collective input of the entire community. Leaders must create opportunities for ongoing dialogue and feedback. Establishing and reinforcing shared values within an administrative team are essential for fostering a positive and collaborative work environment. Shared values act as a guiding framework for decision-making, shaping daily interactions and creating a unified sense of purpose among team members. To ensure these values are meaningful, administrators should actively engage their teams in identifying core values and integrating them into everyday operations.

Step 4: Present the Operations Manual

Now that you've developed the manual with your staff, present the completed document. Leaders should review each section of the PPM in detail. Once finalized, send the revised and final draft to staff. This document reflects the collective approach on how you have agreed to navigate situations and scenarios as an office. Once the final draft is sent, set a deadline and request a written acknowledgment and response of receipt of the policy.

Step 5: Create Plan for Ongoing Maintenance, Modifications, and Recertification

Finally, administrators can implement continuous improvement cycles by incorporating regular feedback loops and evaluation mechanisms. Conducting quarterly reviews of office hours, flexible work arrangements, and meeting structures—using anonymous feedback forms or team discussions—can help leaders assess effectiveness and pinpoint areas for improvement. Leaders can pose the following questions to their team to gain feedback:

- What challenges or bottlenecks have you encountered in current policy and procedures? Do you have suggestions for improvement?
- Are there any policies or procedures you feel are outdated or unclear? What additional guidance or updates might be helpful?
- What successful practices or workflow improvements have you implemented this year that are not yet reflected in our policies and procedures manual? How can we integrate these into our standard processes?
- Are there any changes in institutional, divisional, or federal/state policies that should be reflected in our manual? If so, how do you suggest we incorporate them?

By continuously refining the policy, administrators can ensure it remains fair, transparent, and supportive of staff needs and operational demands (Haar & Spell, 2004). Leaders should be prepared to make adjustments based on these evaluations, whether revising workflows, addressing underperformance, or celebrating operational successes.

Policy as a Reflection of Values: Themes to Consider in Policy Development Process

In creating these policies, it's important to draw connections to policy development, implementation, and the impact on culture.

The process and how it's approached with staff impacts the workspace and provides insight into a leader's management style and the type of culture they would like to create for the team. Since the development process includes a collaborative approach for staff feedback, this intentionality can reflect values driving policy approaches to development implementation.

The first infrastructure component provided us a tool to assess our professional values. Ultimately, those values will inform how we lead. While the process of policy development can be transactional, it's important to learn that policy creation has the potential to be transformative. As a result, the policy (and policy development process) can directly impact staff morale, job satisfaction, and turnover. Indeed, the authors assert that while parameters are necessary, a PPM should not be too rigid or instructional.

Administrators should incorporate discussions of values into team meetings, performance reviews, and professional development activities. Leaders can keep these principles at the forefront of the team's actions by highlighting how values are applied in daily work and celebrating achievements that reflect them. Encouraging team members to share their experiences related to these values further deepens commitment and understanding (Goffee & Jones, 1996). Here are some examples of guiding philosophies that can inform and guide the decisions for the internal operations manual:

- Fairness and Accountability
- Diversity, Equity, Inclusion (DEI)
- Transparency
- Flexibility
- Work–Life Harmony
- Health and Wellness

The final case study provides an example of how values can guide and shape our approach to policy development. Indeed, there may be some limitations within university and state policy, but as leaders and managers, decisions can be guided by values to document internal operations. In this case study, we present an example of applying a university leave request policy toward developing a PPM. Next, this section applies a values-driven approach to unpack how policy and values conflict or interact.

Case Study 5: Balancing Guiding Philosophies and Operational Needs with Paid Time Off

You are the director of Alumni Affairs at a four-year institution. One day, you examine the leave request for paid time off (PTO) for your staff of four. Three direct reports have requested 40 hours of leave in the middle of October. Upon reviewing the calendar, you realize this is the week of homecoming. Indeed, there is a high office operational need, but there is a conflict of the guiding value of supporting team work–life harmony. Simultaneously, as a manager, you understand the demands of the office this week will not be met. Unfortunately, all time off requests cannot be approved.

In developing this internal policy, the following values of transparency, flexibility, work–life harmony, and DEI will guide the policy formation process to support staff office operation needs.

Transparency

A well-structured policy ensures that staff can manage their work–life harmony while maintaining the continuity of administrative functions. The internal PPM can guide for critical periods (which may include holiday breaks). Guidance regarding the use of PTO during critical periods and institutional breaks can include suggestions on timelines for advance notice or even blackout dates where the office has a high operational need.

Flexibility

Balancing staff needs with operational requirements requires administrators to set fair and consistent criteria for approving leave requests. Administrators should develop a coverage plan that includes cross-training team members, reallocating tasks, or utilizing temporary staff or student workers to manage workloads when employees are on leave.

Work–Life Harmony

Supporting the staff in achieving healthy work–life harmony is a key consideration in developing a leave request policy. Under a guiding philosophy of work–life balance, a rigid approach to approving PTO requests is not recommended. Instead, a policy will emphasize critical periods in advance while allowing for exceptions on a case-by-case basis.

Diversity, Equity, and Inclusion

Leading with DEI as a guiding philosophy requires cultural awareness, such as recognizing that a staff member may need time off for cultural or religious reasons, like Indigenous Peoples Day, Yom Kippur, or Ramadan. A PPM leave policy with blackout days that do not consider these factors can create tension and conflict with values. By anticipating potential conflicts, you, as a leader, can proactively plan and foster belonging in the workplace.

Conclusion of Values-Driven Policy

Administrators should regularly assess their impact on culture and performance to ensure that shared values continue to effectively guide management decisions and the team. By continuously evaluating and refining the application of shared values, administrators ensure they remain relevant and effective in guiding the team's actions and decisions. This ongoing commitment to values-driven leadership creates a resilient and adaptable team capable of navigating challenges and achieving long-term success (Northouse, 2016).

Conclusion

This chapter has explored the importance of setting clear communication expectations, fostering shared values among administrative teams, and implementing transparent leave request policies. These components are essential to creating a cohesive and efficient administrative environment where staff feel supported and valued. By focusing on practical strategies that blend structure with flexibility, higher education administrators can create a responsive and effective operational framework that meets the institution's immediate needs and supports long-term success. Additionally, this chapter explored the importance of setting clear communication expectations, fostering shared values among administrative teams, and implementing transparent leave request policies. These components are essential to creating a cohesive and efficient administrative environment where staff feel supported and valued. By operationalizing these strategies—leveraging technology, standardizing policies, maintaining flexibility, streamlining onboarding, and fostering continuous improvement—administrators can create a more efficient, collaborative, and adaptive higher education environment to support long-term success.

References

Goffee, R., & Jones, G. (1996, November–December). What holds the modern company together. *Harvard Business Review.* https://mgeiscee.wordpress.com/wp-content/uploads/2010/01/b5-goffee.pdf

Haar, J. M., & Spell, C. S. (2004). Program knowledge and value of work-family practices and organizational commitment. *International Journal of Human Resource Management*, 15(6), 1040–1055.

Northouse, P. G. (2016). *Leadership: Theory and practice* (7th ed.). Sage.

Appendix

Sample Table of Contents for a PPM

Table of Contents

Heading	Content
Office Hours	Days and times the office should be open and ready to receive walk-ins, phone calls, and emails
Customer Service Schedule	Established coverage for receiving walk-ins, phone calls, and emails to also include backups and several levels of coverage in the event of an absence (or multiple absences)

(continued)

Table of Contents

Heading	Content
Departmental Schedule	A calendar that outlines relevant routine staff information, including recurring meetings, remote days, events, student worker schedules, etc.
On-Boarding Policies	A list of relevant institutional policies and relevant internal memos that guide the day-to-day operation.
Expectations	An opportunity to discuss ways of proactively working together as a team.
Leave Request Policy	Using the university policy to outline further ways of requesting leave with the supervisor.
Internal Communication	The selection of one primary communication platform, set up of teams, chats, and channels, along with agreed-upon expectations for being online and accessible.
Emails	A way to set expectations on general time frames to respond to internal, external, and student-facing emails.
Deadlines	For recurring and ad hoc projects, it helps establish ways of proactively communicating anticipated completion times if/when a determined deadline cannot be met by the assigned agreed-upon time.
Voicemails	A way to set expectations on general time frames to respond to internal, external, and student-facing voicemails.
Mail	Instructions for incoming and outgoing mail to ensure continuity of interdepartmental mail and external mail. This can be particularly important for confidential or time-sensitive documents (i.e., scholarship materials for a deadline or transcript).
Parking	It includes instructions for staff parking but is mostly directed at instructions for guiding office guests, visitors, appointments, and students to parking in your office. This may include parking codes, tickets, specific parking spots, or ways of validating (along with explicit directions for walking, public transportation, ride sharing, and/or motor vehicles).
Lost & Found	If an item of high value or low value is found in the office, this section outlines appropriate steps for staff to take to secure the item and protect the staff.
Flex Time	This space can outline general approaches to planning flexible time for potential work schedules that fall outside of traditional office hours (e.g., nights and weekends).

Table of Contents

Heading	Content
Dress Code	The university policy will outline a dress code for all staff. This document may help clarify department-specific dress code expectations for specific events on or off campus relevant to the unit (for example, university polo for student affairs, black tie for alumni at an annual gala, or shirt and tie for an MBA admissions recruitment event).
Seasonal Dress Code	In some cases or geographical areas, a different dress code may apply in summer or winter, providing alternative dress code suggestions for the region. Some may even include "casual Friday" or "school spirit Friday" or provide more casual guidelines when academic classes are not in session.

7

Navigating Organizational Structure, Roles, and Staffing Changes

Tracy Pascua Dea

INTRODUCTION

All organizations, whether you realize it or not, have an organizational chart that provides an explanation of workflow and responsibilities. An organizational chart (or org chart) provides a visual map of an organization's internal structure and hierarchy, individual employee function, roles and responsibilities, and lines of authority. At the university level, an organizational chart may include positions such as president, vice president, and dean. At the divisional level, an organizational chart may include positions such as director, assistant director, and coordinator. Regardless of where one falls, organizational charts often include position name, individual currently filling the role, lines to indicate relationships and a brief overview of job duties. They also act as a day-to-day guide to govern employee tasks, interactions, and reporting.

Leaders create and employ org charts because they outline how activities are organized and provide a clear mechanism for employees to obtain help. An effective organizational structure promotes clarity, transparency, efficient decision-making, collaboration and coordination, and accountability. It also enhances efficiency, engaged collaboration, and fulfillment of their mission (Catindig et al., 2024).

This chapter will discuss common organizational chart types and reporting structures, roles and responsibilities, and navigating staff turnover in higher education.

Organizational Chart Types and Reporting Structures

An organizational chart represents the flow of authority, responsibility, and communication with multiple levels, extends downward or across, and allows departments to navigate the often complex nature of an organization (Lassl, 2020). While there are an infinite number of organizational charts in higher education (you'll be hard-pressed to find two that are the same), this chapter will review four types: hierarchical, flat, functional, and matrix (see Figure 7.1).

Hierarchical

A hierarchical structure has a direct chain of command from the top of the organization to the bottom. Visually, the structure often mimics that of a pyramid, with direct reports branching from their supervisors (see Figure 7.2).

At the top there is typically one level, which includes an executive leader. In most higher education institutions, this is often the president, chancellor, or board of trustees. The subsequent tier usually includes vice presidents/provosts, followed by assistant vice presidents/provosts, department head/chairs, directors, assistant directors, and so forth. The bottom level of hierarchical structures typically includes employees who do not directly supervise other individuals. Advantages of a hierarchical structure include clear levels of authority, strong control,

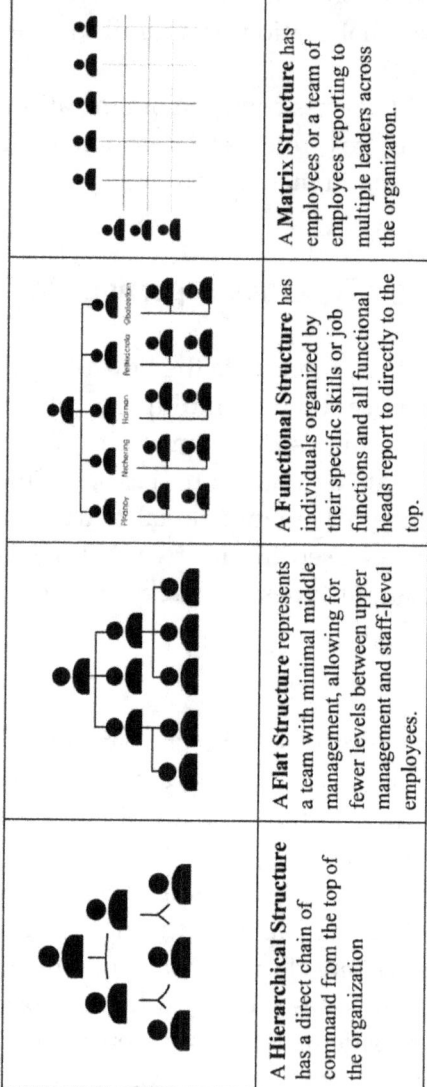

FIGURE 7.1 The Four Organizational Structures.

FIGURE 7.2 Hierarchical Structure.

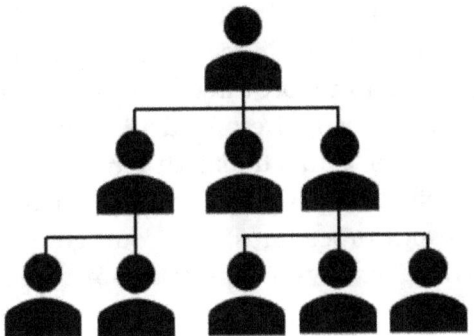

FIGURE 7.3 Flat Structure.

and potential promotion opportunities as employees advance through different levels. However, it can lead to slower decision-making processes as various levels may need to be consulted. There may also be few opportunities for collaboration across levels of the organization.

Flat

A flat structure represents a team with minimal middle management, allowing for fewer levels between upper management and staff-level employees. Middle managers are often in charge of a group of people or department(s) but are not in charge of the whole organization (see Figure 7.3).

Within higher education organizations, middle managers may possess the titles of assistant or associate director, although titles may vary. Visually, the organizational chart is more horizontal. Advantages of a flat structure allows for employees to have more responsibility; it fosters open and streamlined communication and strengthens the adoption of new ideas. However, there is the potential for power struggles within a team or confusion in the absence of clearly defined roles with limited promotion prospects.

Functional

A functional structure is primarily a vertical structure with a clear chain of command to the top (see figure 7.4). Next, individuals are organized by their specific skills or job functions. All functional supervisors report directly to a centrally designated lead (division-head, dean, vice-president, or president).

An advantage of a functional structure is standardization of process, efficiency, centralized decision-making, and clear planning, rules and procedures. It encourages specialization of skills and allows those with expertise to excel and perform at

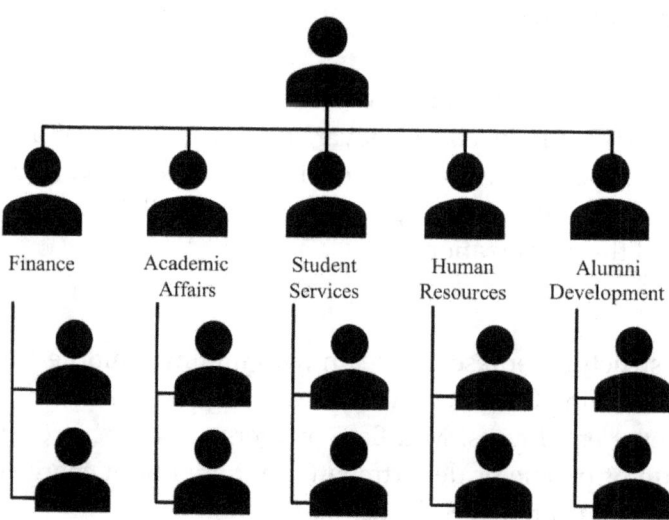

FIGURE 7.4 Functional Structure.

high levels. However, due to the hierarchical decision-making structures and procedures, inadvertent delays and barriers can occur. Further, silos can be created impeding cross-functional collaboration, flexibility, and innovation.

Matrix

A matrix organizational structure means that employees or a team of employees report to multiple leaders across the organization. A matrix structure is a combination of horizontal and vertical structures illustrating in-depth relationships between employees and visually representing a grid (see Figure 7.5). In addition to dual reporting structures, it often allows members from different departments to work together on specific goals.

An advantage of a matrix structure allows for a more dynamic use of employees, allowing them to use their skill set in various capacities. It allows supervisors to select individuals based on the needs of a project. However, it can include potential friction between the managers (e.g., department versus project). Additionally, constant adjustments may need to be made based on ever changing organization needs and projects.

Determining the best type of structure for your department depends upon the state of the organization, employee workforce, resources, and needs. A department in an early stage may require a hierarchical structure while a more established division may

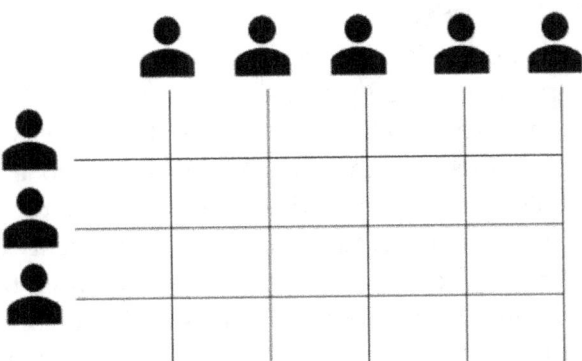

FIGURE 7.5 Matrix Structure.

use a flat or matrix structure. The Appendix outlines the steps a leader can take when creating an organizational chart.

Roles and Responsibilities

With a clearer understanding of the purpose and types of organizational structures in higher education, the focus now shifts to how leaders manage roles and responsibilities. The following strategies may be helpful to leaders managing the process.

Creating Job Descriptions

Each managed position should have an accompanied detailed job description that outlines the essential functions, reporting relationships, required qualifications, and compensation levels. For new positions, you may need to create a job description that defines the above from scratch. For existing positions, job descriptions may already be documented and on file with human resources. It's an effective practice to review similar roles at other institutions to ensure your approach is in line with industry standards. A well-crafted argument, supported by data, staffing plans, and organizational and strategic goals, can help you effectively communicate your needs to your supervisor, particularly during a hiring freeze or when advocating for additional resources.

Establishing Role Clarity

In addition to possessing an established organizational chart, it is equally important that employees have a strong understanding of their job responsibilities and expectations. This allows them to recognize how their work contributes to the overall organization's goals. Role clarity creates a clear definition of an employee's responsibilities and helps to prevent confusion, enhances job satisfaction, and ensures that all within the organization are aligned and working toward common objectives. Role clarity can be achieved by having accurate job descriptions or defined and documented responsibilities. It can also assist others in understanding the roles and responsibilities of your staff and your functional area.

Reviewing Job Descriptions

Leaders should review job descriptions on a regular basis for accuracy. Additionally, involving staff members in this review can be a welcomed practice. Prior to sharing the job description on file with human resources, ask your direct reports to curate a bullet pointed list of day-to-day responsibilities, major goals, and work-related outputs. A leader may ask employees, "what are your key tasks each day?" or "how do these tasks or functions contribute to the departmental mission?" After working several years in a department, individuals may experience additional responsibilities being added to their role, which may be undocumented. Accountability and communication channels may also be informal and blurred. This process provides a leader and other stakeholders an understanding of needs in relation to departmental goals. Further, the process can lead to the identification of gaps or overlaps in responsibilities.

Once revised, share the updated job description and defined roles with department employees and other stakeholders with whom you often collaborate. Providing capacity-building exercises, training, and coaching further helps individuals fully understand their roles and responsibilities while also prioritizing professional growth and development (see Chapter 8).

Promotion Within the Organization

Creating well-defined roles and responsibilities allows leaders (and employees) to see pathways for promotion and growth within a department. With access to clear and documented roles, responsibilities, and organizational charts, employees can readily understand opportunities and familiarize themselves with roles of interest and the skills and qualifications needed to pursue a role. They can seek out opportunities to engage in professional development (e.g., certifications, conferences, mentorship) and other continuous learning opportunities to develop the knowledge and skills necessary to advance their career (see Chapter 8).

By utilizing these strategies, employees gain clarity on their daily tasks, a sense of confidence in their roles, and avoid performing superfluous tasks. In times of unanticipated change, these exercises can also serve as a valuable tool for maintaining stability.

Navigating Staff Turnover

Research from the College and University Professional Association for Human Resources (CUPA-HR, 2023) reports that turnover in higher education is at an all-time high. Findings indicated an increase in turnover among both exempt and non-exempt staff. For exempt staff, turnover has increased from 7.9% in 2017–2018 to 14.3% in 2022–2023. During the same period, non-exempt staff turnover increased from 9.4% to 15.2%. Additionally, the number was even higher for student affairs–related areas, in which close to 40% of professionals indicated they were likely to search for a new role within the next year. Reasons cited across all groups included poor job satisfaction, low compensation, burnout, and limited opportunities for career advancement (Trower, 2019). Challenges discussed here will continue to remain for the foreseeable future. Therefore, it is critically important that leaders are prepared to navigate staff turnover within their own units and divisions.

Documenting Processes

In addition to revising and updating job descriptions and establishing role clarity, leaders should encourage employees to document programs, processes, and procedures necessary to perform their job. Employees should seek to capture all the necessary steps needed to perform a task or execute a program in their absence. This can be done via written documents saved on a local computer drive, a shared Google Drive or process document software such as Scribe or Document360. Documenting processes will mitigate challenges often associated with turnover, such as the loss of organizational knowledge.

Transition Planning

While planning for departures, whether expected or unexpected, leaders must also consider the impact the departure will have on their immediate team.

For some, the staff member may be highly respected with lots of connections within the team. For others, the departure may be welcomed news as the person has been disruptive to team culture. In either case, you'll have to make decisions regarding messaging, timelines, and next steps. Be prepared to answer questions surrounding where the employee is going, who will pick up their remaining work, and plans for the future of the team or department (especially if the person who is leaving is a direct supervisor of other professional staff members). It is important to listen to your remaining team members and reinforce opportunities that may exist as a result of this individual's departure (e.g., internal promotions, recruitment, reorganization, etc.). You can work with your direct report in their remaining time at the organization to help them have a smooth departure. This includes navigating human resources–related tasks, such as equipment returns and work-related reassignments.

Conclusion

This chapter described the importance and purpose of having a clear organizational structure within your unit or division. It also provided leaders with examples of commonly utilized structures as well as common roles found in the collegiate context. An audit, conducted in conjunction with your team, may assist you in the development and/or revision of your organizational chart, current staffing levels, and roles and responsibilities of each team member. As the field of higher education adapts to the proliferation of online education, changing student demographics, and higher levels of accountability in student learning outcomes, organizational structures and cultures must adapt to facilitate continued growth and success.

References

Catindig, R.G., Matriano, E.A., & Bueno, D.C. (2024). Exploring the benefits of a lean, efficient, and effective organizational structure of a graduate school. *Institutional Multidisciplinary Research and Development Journal, 7*(10), 33–48.

CUPA-HR. (2023, April). *The Higher Ed Admissions Workforce.* www.cupahr.org/surveys/research-briefs/the-higher-ed-admissions-workforce-april-2023/

Lassl, W. (2020). *The viability of organizations: Vol. 3. Designing and changing organizations.* Springer. https://doi.org/10.1007/978-3-030-61446-1.

Trower, C.A. (2019). Faculty and staff turnover in higher education: The role of workload and workplace stress. *New Directions for Higher Education, 2019*(188), 27–37.

Appendix

Creating an Organizational Chart

There are several steps to consider when creating an organizational chart. The following six steps will help you get started.

1. Define the Purpose
    - Determine the goal of the chart, e.g., department structure, role clarity, project team
    - Decide how much detail is needed, e.g., macro-level or big picture information or micro-level or detailed
2. Gather Information
    - Collect data on employees, roles, reporting relationships
    - Identify key positions, functions, subunits, or areas
    - Determine how individuals or teams collaborate and interact
3. Choose an Organizational Chart Type
    - Select a structure based on needs and purpose, e.g., hierarchical, flat, functional, matrix
    - Choose a tool for drafting the chart, e.g., paper, whiteboard, software

4. Build the Chart
   - Start with the highest role at the top, e.g., director, dean
   - Connect direct reports or any reporting relationships using lines or similar connectors
   - Group any similar roles or units together
   - Use consistent shapes, colors, or other symbols to provide clarity
5. Review and Gather Feedback
   - Verify accuracy with key stakeholders or leaders
   - Ensure names, titles, and reporting relationships are accurate
   - Make any adjustments based on feedback
6. Share and Maintain
   - Distribute the chart, making it easy to accessible on an internal website or shared drive
   - Regularly review and update the chart to reflect any changes

8

Training and Development: The Keys to Building Successful and Sustainable Teams

Nicole Caridad Ralston, Kevin Lewis, and Shawn Gaines

INTRODUCTION

We have all been there, right? You have entered a new phase of your professional journey and are now expected to manage fellow humans. Or perhaps you have accepted a new position that oversees a division in which you are responsible for supervising assistant deans and directors. Your first thought might be excitement or sheer terror. Managing people is hard. Full stop. Period. One of the crucial aspects of managing a group of people is training and developing them into a strong team of individuals who center excellence and accountability in the workplace.

Shortly after transitioning from a ten-year career in higher education and student affairs, Dr. Ralston was tasked with hiring, training, and developing a department at a young nonprofit, Beloved Community. This racial and economic equity consulting organization offers individualized services and consulting to schools and workplaces committed to advancing their equity journey. At the time, she hired four associate directors who served as curriculum designers, consultants, and facilitators for clients. Five years later, due to increased demand, this team rapidly expanded to a team of nine. The success of that team's growth is firmly rooted in Beloved Community's commitment to training and development. Using first-hand experience, this chapter will discuss onboarding, training and development, and performance management practices utilized to achieve success.

Onboarding

The onboarding period for new staff is a pivotal time to ensure that they understand the values, philosophy, and expectations at your organization and on your team. It also begins the trust-building process that is imperative for managers and staff in the workplace. Employees who have a positive experience with onboarding report higher job satisfaction levels and clearer understandings of their roles (Renn & Hodges, 2007).

When hiring new team members, it's essential to ensure they are set up for success from the start. Appendix A provides a sample onboarding agenda for your review. In a study conducted by Sapling HR, a People Operations Platform, the average new employee is expected to complete 54 activities during their onboarding process (Oak, n.d.). Examples include having keys ready, access forms completed, email activated, directions to their reporting location, and any other relevant information they may need. Unfortunately, in Dr. Ralston's first professional role in higher education, there was no clear onboarding process. She did not know where to park, how to log into her computer, where various campus offices were located, and was not given so much as an introduction to the unit. There was no written or formal training, agenda, or documents. This made it extremely difficult to transition into the role and created a great sense of dissonance between her personal values and organizational culture. As a leader, it is your job to ensure a seamless onboarding process that meets an individual's needs. Appendix A provides a sample onboarding agenda.

Training and Development

While onboarding and training is specific and focuses on job- specific-related tasks, professional development refers to a broader, ongoing process that helps to advance one's career. Examples may include pursuing advanced education, attending a local or national conference, or seeking mentorship, all of which can improve and expand expertise beyond one's current role. It is a lifelong learning process that promotes engagement with the latest best practices of one's chosen field. Some aspects of professional development include identifying goals, developing a plan and competencies needed to succeed, creating an individualized development plan and, finally, receiving feedback. For new employees, training can assist them in adjusting to their new job. Examples include terms of employment, policies, norms, values, etc. For seasoned employees, training can be used as an opportunity to teach or reinforce skills and desired behaviors. As a leader, the promotion of training and professional development amongst your team demonstrates to employees you are invested in their success and advancement. This section will outline some ways of assessing each team member's professional development and training needs and compare those to your team needs. Next, this section will include strategies for infusing professional development into your team's annual calendar. The third part will outline accountability measures for professional development to ensure consistent emphasis on growth and self-awareness. Lastly, this section will discuss the importance of developing your own competencies as a leader.

Assess Team Training and Professional Development

To determine areas of development for your staff, direct your attention to what employees are constantly asking for support within their day-to-day duties. Are they constantly asking for strategies to manage their time on long-term projects? If so, perhaps you could consider project management or time management team training. Are they often asking you how to deliver difficult feedback to their peers? If so, perhaps you could consider a team training dedicated to candid conversations, navigating conflict, and giving feedback. Additionally, you may gain information from candid conversations with your employees during one-on-one conversations and competency reviews. You can use this information to suggest opportunities for development. Lastly, as a leader, you may choose to administer a survey or assessment to collect information. The use of a Google form can create and structure questions to anonymously solicit feedback from staff. Staff may be more comfortable sharing confidentiality. Information gathered can be used to assess their levels of comfort with technology or knowledge of processes.

Strategies for Addressing Staff Training and Development

As a consideration, budgets may vary across institutions; therefore, funding for professional development may not be readily available and accessible. However, the authors outline several strategies that leaders can use to develop professional development pathways.

Internal Trainings

Internal training uses the organization's own resources and expertise to equip employees with the work-related skills and knowledge needed to excel in their roles. Internal training can be delivered in a variety of ways, including workshops, online courses, or one-on-one coaching sessions. This can be from a supervisor, colleague, or an expert on campus who possess specialized knowledge in a relevant subject area. For example, you may use your weekly staff meeting to invite a campus partner to speak on various resources, programs, and services available to students. Alternatively, you could schedule time with your enrollment manager to discuss the student body composition and brainstorm mechanism by which students can be retained. Staff members can share their expertise by teaching topics in which they are proficient. Another valuable approach is to organize quarterly or semester retreats, where staff can bond, enhance communication, and develop key skills in a collaborative environment. Internal training can be more cost-effective compared to external training.

External Trainings

External training occurs when individuals or a group of individuals from outside the organization are brought in to deliver training on a specific topic or skill. While these external trainers may have limited knowledge of the organization itself, they bring deep expertise in their subject area. Some examples include the use of race in admissions, customer service, or innovative teaching strategies. This provides employees with an opportunity to break out of traditional training models and gain fresh perspectives. However, utilizing external trainers or attending a conference requires funding, which should be covered by the organization.

Cross-Training

One effective approach to staff training is through the use of cross-training. When implemented collaboratively and thoughtfully, it allows staff members to shadow colleagues performing different functions or working in other departments. In this manner, staff are able to receive an overview or learn the job functions and responsibilities of another employee. It fosters an appreciation for others' roles and enables staff to answer basic questions more effectively.

Protect Team Time

Professional development and training does not always occur in group settings, but can also exist as a self-navigated exercise. Managers can support this approach by establishing calendar holds. Managers can protect two to four hours every quarter for the team's training needs. These team step-back days allow the team to step away from their typical duties. These days are also essential for sharing best practices amongamong team members, relationship building, and illustrating that there is an expectation (and support) for continuous improvement.

Professional Resources

There are a wealth of resources available on professional development in the form of newsletters, blogs, and webinars. To support a culture of professional development, encourage subscriptions to industry publications while also sharing those webinars and engagement opportunities of specific interest to your team.

Conference Attendance

Leaders can support their staff in encouraging them to attend local or national conferences that align with their interest and/or area of desired growth. These events not only offer educational sessions but also opportunities to network, learn specialized knowledge and skills, and engage in career development. Staff can take notes and return to the organization to report back on what they have learned.

The strategies presented above serve as a starting guide for leaders to think about the ways in which they can train and develop their teams. These formal and informal processes are at the foundation of all successful organizations. It is a continuous process as needs shift, new systems are utilized, and environmental contexts change.

Inclusive Performance Management

The University of Kansas' Human Resources Department defines performance management as, "an on-going, continuous process of communicating and clarifying job responsibilities, priorities, performance expectations, and development planning that optimize an individual's performance and aligns with organizational strategic goals" (University of Kansas, n.d.). Oftentimes, it includes goal-setting (i.e., planning), monitoring (i.e., feedback), and evaluation (i.e., appraising). These evaluations, typically conducted in a one-on-one meeting with a supervisor, allow for the opportunity to present feedback regarding job performance and evaluate employee performance against expected job outcomes. Ultimately, this section will frame how to build healthy feedback practices that allow you to address, celebrate and, if necessary, correct employee performance. Appendix B provides an outline for performance management within your organization.

Establishing an inclusive performance management system involves aligning your team, campus, and organizational values with the purpose of performance management. Without having a process for employee performance management, there may be few times available to provide feedback on job performance. Performance evaluations are a method that can be used as a mechanism to engage employees regarding work-related performance and objectives. As a result, employees will have a better understanding of what is expected of them, how performance is measured, and, finally, any opportunities for growth that may be available with the organization. It also serves as an important tool that is connected to incentive and discipline processes. Providing feedback the first time should not be in the evaluation process. Rather, the evaluation is a summation of past performance and assumes check-ins have occurred over time. For example, you should not wait until an employee is disregarding organizational values and norms, failing to complete expected job outcomes, or has become apathetic in their role.

Once there is an understanding of the need for performance evaluations, we turn our attention to the tools at your disposal for guiding this process.

Probationary Period Review

Typically, organizations hire employees under a probationary period to ensure they are capable of expected job outcomes. These can range between 30 and 60 days or six months to a year. As a suggestion, leaders should develop clear rubrics outlining expectations of the employee. This provides an opportunity for the staff member and manager to check in throughout the probationary period to ensure expectations are being met. If, at the end of a probationary period, they are not performing to the expectations of the manager, they may be released from employment. However, it is important to acknowledge that these probationary periods may not be enough time for an employee to appropriately transition and learn the skills and strategies needed to be successful within the organization.

Quarterly and Yearly Performance Evaluations

Most institutions conduct performance evaluations annually but leaders should consider doing them more frequently. They are typically based in three primary functions: the assessment of employee performance, the distribution of workload, and the determination of the direction of employee development. These evaluations can identify and reward effective employees and outline plans for improving underperformance of those that are not meeting expectations. They are carried out by the employee's immediate supervisor and are often more formalized against a set of performance metrics. Finally, it should be impartial and objective, which can be accomplished through the use of strictly defined criteria. As a leader, we recommend four quarterly evaluations as opposed to one yearly evaluation. To remind both employee and manager, placing a reminder on calendars may be beneficial.

360-Degree Review

The 360-degree review allows team members to receive feedback from not only their manager, but also from their colleagues. In this process, each team member reviews themselves in self-reflection, receives feedback from their colleagues, and receives feedback from their manager. Multi-rater feedback practices allow leaders to gather insight from multiple sources. As a manager, you are then responsible for reviewing all of the feedback, finding themes and outliers in the feedback, and delivering the complete feedback package to your direct report. The 360 review helps an individual or a team understand what they should keep doing and where they can improve. However, the 360-degree evaluation has been critiqued for inexperienced or subjective reviewers and a focus on employee weaknesses rather than strengths.

Performance Improvement Plan (PIP)

A performance improvement plan (PIP) is a tool that is typically used to outline an area of concern, narrates the concrete changes and goals that must be met, and offers training and resources to return an employee to good standing. The PIP should be rooted in job competencies and organizational values or expectations. PIP timelines may vary, but typically allow for at least 30 days for employees to make requested changes. Additionally, they can sometimes be employed as a last-chance effort for a direct report to improve performance.

Conclusion

In conclusion, navigating the complexities of managing a team is both a challenging and rewarding journey. By prioritizing onboarding, training and development, professional development, and inclusive performance evaluation, you create an environment where individuals can thrive and contribute their unique strengths. When you invest in your team's growth and foster a culture of transparency and trust, the potential for success is boundless. As you embark on your leadership journey, we hope you carry forward these insights, learning from both successes and challenges, to build a resilient and dynamic team that champions both excellence and accountability.

References

Oak. (n.d.). Employee onboarding statistics. Retrieved November 1, 2024, from www.oak.com/blog/employee-onboarding-statistics/

Renn, K. A., & Hodges, J. (2007). The first year on the job: Experiences of new professionals in student affairs. *Journal of Student Affairs Research and Practice*, 44(2), 604–628. https://doi.org/10.2202/1949-6605.1800

University of Kansas. (n.d.). Performance management. Retrieved November 1, 2024, from https://humanresources.ku.edu/performance-management

Appendix A

Sample Onboarding Agenda

- Onboarding Preparation
  - Send welcome email with essential first-day information
  - Prepare workspace
  - Set up email and system access
- First-Day Activities
  - Welcome meeting with supervisor
  - Welcome meeting with team
  - Office/campus tour
- Administrative Tasks
  - Complete human resource paperwork
  - Set up direct deposit and payroll information
  - Review organizational structure and policies
- Training and Resources
  - Attend/design orientation sessions covering institutional mission and values
  - Review key student affairs competencies
  - Familiarize with relevant software and databases
  - Discuss existing workflows
- Review of Essential Documents
  - Review organizational and departmental charts
  - Read strategic plans and goals
  - Familiarize with departmental handbooks and guidelines
  - Review student support services available on campus
- 30-Day Checklist
  - Schedule one-on-one meetings with team members
  - Participate in team-building activities or social events
  - Conduct informational interviews with key stakeholders
  - Meet with the supervisor to clarify job expectations
  - Review and discuss the 30-60-90-day plan/rubric
  - Shadow colleagues in various roles
  - Understand roles and responsibilities
  - Identify training opportunities or workshops to attend
  - Start working on a personal development plan aligned with professional competencies

- 60-Day Checklist
  - Continue to meet with colleagues and mentors
  - Attend campus events or departmental meetings
  - Participate in student engagement activities
  - Begin applying learned skills in practical scenarios (advising sessions, program planning)
  - Review progress with the supervisor and adjust goals as needed
  - Solicit feedback from peers and supervisors on performance and integration
  - Reflect on experiences and identify areas for further growth
- 90-Day Checklist
  - Conduct a review with the supervisor to assess progress against the 30-60-90-day plan
  - Engage in a project that connects with the wider campus community
  - Identify opportunities for leadership roles within student affairs
  - Update the User Guide based on experiences and preferences
  - Share insights and experiences in team meetings to foster a collaborative culture

Appendix B

Performance Management Outline

- Define Performance Management
  - Clearly articulate what performance management means for your team
  - Ensure all team members understand the connection to organizational goals
  - Identify your organization's core values (e.g., transparency, accountability)
  - Ground performance evaluations in documented behaviors and specific competencies
- Onboarding Integration
  - Develop an onboarding module that includes performance management expectations
  - Introduce key performance management tools

- Conduct 30-60-90-Day Evaluation
  - Create a detailed rubric outlining performance expectations for the first 90 days
  - Ensure accountability measures are included for ongoing performance assessment
- Quarterly/Yearly Evaluation
  - Determine when and how you will assess employee performance, the distribution of workload, and the determination of the direction of employee development
- Implement 360-Degree Reviews
  - Establish a process for conducting 360-degree feedback
  - Provide clear guidelines for self-reflection, peer feedback, and manager evaluations
- 2 x 2 Evaluations
  - Develop 2 x 2 feedback form specific to your organization
  - Set timeline for how often conversations will take place
- Establish Continuous Feedback Loops
  - Schedule regular check-ins (e.g., monthly) for performance discussions
  - Utilize structured feedback forms, such as the 2 x 2 feedback form
- Reflection and Improvement
- Schedule regular reviews of the performance management process to identify areas for improvement
- Gather feedback from team members on the effectiveness of performance management practices

9

Leading Through Effective Communication: Strategies for Collaboration

Christy Heaton and Nick Fuselier

INTRODUCTION

In higher education, the successful exchange of information and collaboration is vital for the success of any organization. Leaders should encourage and foster communication amongst their team, promoting clarity and alignment on complex projects and trust, ultimately leading to efficient problem-solving. For example, a director may need to disseminate information and collaborate with staff related to a campus closure, perhaps due to inclement weather (or other emergency) sharing the ways office operations may be impacted. Communication is the backbone of effective collaboration, enabling individuals to share ideas, coordinate efforts, and work toward a common goal. In the above example, leaders may need to collaborate with campus officials on messaging, programming, staffing, etc. Partnerships can also help reduce redundancy, share resources, and increase productivity.

As higher education institutions adapt to new challenges and opportunities, enhancing communication and collaboration strategies will be critical to maintaining their effectiveness and relevance.

This chapter focuses on considerations related to communication and collaboration for those leading teams and organizations. After defining these concepts in the context of higher education, we examine how leaders can identify internal and external stakeholders. We then offer a discussion of the importance and benefits of effective communication and collaboration. Finally, the chapter concludes with a strategic guide to intentional communication and collaboration that leaders can utilize in their role (see the Appendix).

Terminology

In higher education, leaders must communicate with a diverse range of stakeholders, including faculty, staff, students, alumni, donors, officials, community members, senior leadership, etc. For the purposes of this chapter, we define communication as the ways in which individuals share information, articulate thoughts and ideas, inform, and interact with one another through both verbal and nonverbal methods. Northouse (2016) expanded on this definition, writing that, "communication is the vehicle through which leaders and followers create, nurture, and sustain useful exchanges" (p. 146). It can occur through a number of channels, including, but not limited to face-to-face meetings, town halls, emails, social media, presentations, etc. Although elements of communication are naturally embedded in all administrative work, a focus on clear, consistent, and effective communication is key to a leader's success. It is essential to build strong relationships, foster collaboration and ensure the success and advancement of their department, division, and institution.

Collaboration across departments and institutions has tremendous benefits for both students and the institution. It is a necessary organizational process that spans across institutional functions, often including program administration, strategic planning, leadership practices, accountability mechanisms, and decision-making (Morris & Miller-Stevens, 2016). Collaboration includes the joint contributions of individuals or individual units to share in the planning, coordination, implementation, and assessment of an institution's array of operations. For students, collaboration can create a seamless learning experience. For institutions, collaboration can lead to improved efficiency and effectiveness.

Identifying Internal and External Constituents

Due to the very nature of communication and collaboration, specifically their direct dependence on establishing relationships with others, it is useful to examine how a leader can identify internal and external stakeholders.

Internally, it should be no surprise that leaders often communicate and collaborate regularly with student workers, staff, and leaders in their department and division. Similarly, leaders must also ensure that other departments and senior administration are updated. Ensuring that stakeholders are kept informed lays the groundwork for greater operational efficiency, better decision-making, and stronger relationships throughout the organization. Leading a department also requires effective collaboration with campus partners to accomplish goals. This can involve sharing of data sets, collaborating on events, or unifying budgets/resources to advance projects or goals. To initiate effective communication and collaboration, leaders can identify key individuals and campus partners by reviewing the organizational chart of their department and institution (see Chapter 7). This exercise helps leaders understand how information flows and presents opportunities for future collaboration. For example, a director of a first-year experience department who understands the organizational chart and mission statements of similar institutional departments may consider academic advising, enrollment management, and institutional research as key campus partners. Partnering together on projects, programs, and services can reduce redundancy, improve efficiency, and enhance student outcomes.

External constituents are off-campus partners/stakeholders who contribute, add value, or impact the success of a unit. Oftentimes, they have the ability to inform or impact strategy. For the admissions office, external constituents may include school counselors, community college advisors, parents/guardians, middle school principals, alumni, and boards of trustees. A starting point for leaders to identify stakeholders may be attached to an institution's context (e.g., alumni, donors, corporate partners), geographic context (e.g., community board), or governance-related stakeholders (e.g., board of trustees). Although external constituents are often off-campus, their influence on an institution's success remains strong.

Leaders should consider the following when attempting to identify constituents:

- **Who**: Identify individuals that have a stake in the information or the collaboration opportunity.
- **How**: Communicate and collaborate with these constituents through various channels, including in person meetings, emails, and Zoom.
- **When**: Communicate the information or the need to collaborate at appropriate times, ensuring timely updates and clear scheduling for meetings and decisions.

Importance of Communication

In higher education, the exchange of information is paramount for the functioning and success of the organization. Additionally, due to the complex nature of institutions, the flow of information impacts learning, research, and administration. Although elements of communication are naturally embedded in all administrative work, a focus on clear, consistent, and effective communication is key to a leader's success. For the purpose of this chapter, the authors intend to focus on the importance of communication for leaders with their teams and senior leadership.

Communication Among Teams

Leaders of all levels should strive to keep their team members informed of expectations, policies and procedures, and key priorities within their department or division. This is due to the fast-paced environments, changing priorities, and shifts in resources or staffing often found within higher education. Therefore, a leader's ability to communicate, adjust, and respond with their team begins with a strong foundation in communication standards. Effective communication reduces redundancy, enhances clarity, and helps set clear expectations. When team members understand the "why" behind their work, they can better align with the broader objectives of the institution. Effective information sharing can also help to increase transparency and trust within teams. By sharing information, it demonstrates to staff members that they are valued and included. However, the authors acknowledge that it is necessary to find an appropriate balance between sharing too little and oversharing. Sharing too little can lead to confusion and oversharing may lead to information overload.

Communicating with Senior Administrators

Effective communication with senior administrators is a crucial skill leaders must possess, as it is essential for ensuring alignment with institutional goals. It also is the mechanism by which administrators gain a better understanding of your department or division, staffing, and resources. By sharing information with your supervisor and other senior administrators, you have the unique opportunity to demonstrate how the unit(s) you oversee contribute to the overall strategic plan and institutional objectives. This has the potential to secure additional resources and strengthen the support they have for your initiatives. Leadership can also play a key role in amplifying your department or division's story, especially when they have a deep knowledge and awareness of the overall contributions being made to advance institutional goals and objectives. Regular communication also creates an opportunity to address any concerns or challenges proactively, rather than letting them escalate.

To communicate effectively with senior administrators, it's important to be clear and concise. Administrators have numerous responsibilities, so being respectful of their time by focusing on the key points is essential. Regular meetings, email updates, or other methods of communication should be determined based on what works best for both parties. In some instances, you might find yourself "managing up." Managing up involves problem-solving, working ahead, and supporting your supervisor on issues or challenges (Joshi et al., 2024). This allows you and your supervisor to partner and create opportunities to better serve your department. The goal is to establish a communication flow that is efficient and effective. By regularly sharing your department's progress and contributions, you ensure that your team is not only recognized but also supported in achieving its goals within the larger institutional framework.

Importance of Collaboration

Collaborations can provide an opportunity to solve challenging problems facing higher education by sharing resources, knowledge, and skills of individual partners to achieve joint goals. Formal collaborations occur when they are mandated, dictated with a clear outcome (e.g., President's Task Force for Campus Safety). Informal collaborations are created organically when two or more individuals or departments join to address a challenge facing both departments (e.g., faculty from different departments team up to co-host a workshop on a topic of mutual interest, such as student engagement strategies). Whether formal or informal, these collaborations often emerge because of mandates from institutions or policymakers, improving student learning outcomes, saving on resources, or obtaining a shared goal. These ventures, whether between or among institutions or departmental programs, can be effective in obtaining operational efficiency.

There are also a number of benefits associated with collaboration. First, collaborations provide an opportunity for individuals and teams to share ideas and best practices, fostering innovation and growth. Collaborations can also engage harder-to-reach groups, such as a partnership between counseling services and athletics that could better support student athletes while promoting mental wellness. Furthermore, collaborations help ease the burden on individuals or smaller departments. Consider for instance, a new student orientation and transition program office with one professional staff member. By collaborating with other departments (e.g., academic advising, university ambassadors, student success), the office can leverage collective resources to execute programming during the first few weeks of the semester. This shared responsibility not only ensures a smoother transition for students but also distributes the workload across multiple departments. By fostering greater alignment between institutions and departments, collaborations create a more cohesive and efficient approach to achieving institutional goals.

While policymakers and funding agencies increasingly emphasize the need to partner, Pamela Eddy, in *Partnerships in Higher Education* (2010) posits that merely dictating it does not predict success. For leaders who choose not to collaborate with others (or do so poorly), they may miss out on important historical and institutional knowledge needed to make decisions that may situate problem-solving in a political, economical, and technological context. Second, there may be negative economic or unrealistic financial implications by not consulting with relevant campus partners when committing the institution to strategies in a silo. Third, leaders may inadvertently negatively impact the operations of other departments. Consider, for example, an enrollment manager who makes the decision to reduce the number of questions on the admissions application in an effort to reduce the amount spent completing the application. In doing so, the decision is made to combine permanent residence and mailing residence addresses. Without discussing this with other departments, this decision has an adverse impact on other campus partners. This includes the registrar, who can no longer determine residency status and the financial aid staff, who now has difficulty creating institutional, state, and national funding packages.

While the importance of communication and collaboration has been established, understanding the practical methods that facilitate these partnerships is key to ensuring they achieve their desired outcomes. In the following section, we will explore strategies that can be employed by leaders and teams to enhance communication and foster meaningful collaborations.

Tools for Effective Communication and Collaboration

We conclude this chapter with some examples of tools leaders can utilize to communicate and collaborate with one another. From in-person interactions to virtual spaces and messaging platforms, communication and collaboration have many vehicles. Exploring and creating a variety of options allow for constituents to voice thoughts, concerns, perspectives, and experiences in a multitude of ways. These tools, when used strategically, can enhance engagement, strengthen relationships, and drive the success of collaborative efforts across teams and departments.

Community Dialogues

Community dialogues are small- to medium-sized gatherings that can be led by one or more facilitators who guide the group's discussion with a series of prompts. A facilitated dialogue can help leaders communicate with their team or brainstorm ideas surrounding a particular collaboration opportunity. Additionally, they can serve as a valuable space to gather feedback at the conclusion of a collaborative project, allowing teams to reflect on what worked well and where improvements can be made for future initiatives.

Focus Groups

Focus groups are small- to medium-sized groups that allow for participants to share ideas and perspectives. These spaces offer a formal and dynamic way for members to express themselves in person or online in real time. By facilitating open discussions, focus groups allow leaders to gain deeper insights into needs, preferences, and potential challenges. The feedback gathered also has the potential to inform future collaboration opportunities.

Infographics

One strategy to highlight your department's work is to create an infographic. These visual representations provide an overview of your department's efforts and achievements over the course of a semester or year. In operationalizing an infographic, leaders may choose to develop one that includes metrics such as number of student meetings, major programs and initiatives, and common topics for which students sought support. Sharing these infographics with other departments can foster collaboration by providing a snapshot of your department's impact, helping to align goals and identify potential areas for collaboration.

Lunch and Learn

Lunch and learn can take place in person or virtually. The atmosphere is typically informal, inviting attendees to bring their lunch and connect. Leadership can share information with staff members while providing an opportunity for them to provide immediate feedback or ask questions. For example, leaders may choose to host a lunch and learn with their staff while watching a relevant webinar hosted by a local or national association on topics related to student needs or success. From a collaboration perspective, these events can also be used to invite colleagues from other departments to share insights and collaborate on initiatives.

Messaging Platforms

Having systems defined for communication in real time can lead to operational efficiency for offices especially when considering alternative work schedules, event-planning in multiple locations, or circumstances that require a rapid response. Messaging platforms, such as Microsoft Teams, Slack, and Google Chat, are online spaces for messaging, sharing ideas, organizing projects, and collaborating. These systems can support a centrally established location for communication and collaboration through instant messaging, file sharing, and integration with other productivity tools to streamline processes. Whether through channels, direct messages, or group chats, these platforms can be an essential tool for keeping individuals connected and organized.

One-on-One Meetings
One-on-one meetings with your staff, supervisor, and senior administrators can serve as an essential part of your communication strategy and a key element in fostering collaboration. These meetings provide a dedicated space to discuss progress on tasks, clarify expectations, and address any challenges. They also serve as a forum for providing professional development. One-on-one meetings are typically structured around an agenda and review previous initiatives, relevant data, upcoming goals, and provide space to discuss pertinent information. When used strategically, these meetings can create opportunities to align efforts, share feedback, and identify areas for collaboration between departments or teams.

Quarterly, Semesterly, and Yearly Reports
These reports are a comprehensive document that outlines the department's achievements, challenges, and progress over a selected period of time. They typically include information related to key metrics, accomplishments, budgetary considerations, and major events or initiatives. The report highlights how the department or division's work aligns with the institution's strategic goals and mission. It serves as both a reflective tool and a communication piece for senior leadership and stakeholders. Additionally, these reports can create opportunities for collaboration by identifying areas of overlap or synergy between departments.

Surveys
Surveys can be useful instruments in collecting feedback from a wide range of individuals in a format that allows members to share anonymously. This format may be more appealing to

some who feel they have less agency to speak freely and openly. Surveys can give a voice to members who might perceive themselves as more vulnerable, and therefore, less likely to share in more public settings. By capturing feedback, surveys can identify common challenges, needs, or interests, which can serve as a foundation for future collaboration. Leaders can use survey results to pinpoint areas where different departments or teams can address shared concerns or enhance existing processes.

Town Halls
Town halls are typically more structured and formal opportunities for engagement.

Typically, these are led by institutional leaders and are intended to be large-group gatherings of members across an institution. Successful town halls tend to be highly structured, allowing adequate time for leaders to communicate about a topic and for attendees to ask questions and express concerns.

Video Conferencing Platforms
Video conferencing platforms, such as Zoom, allow users to host virtual meetings, webinars, and collaborate through video, audio, and chat. They also tend to have features like screen sharing, recording, and breakout rooms. This type of tool can be an integral part of any communication strategy, used to facilitate one-on-one meetings or staff meetings, particularly with remote staff.

Virtual Bulletin Boards
One way that leaders can engage their internal and external stakeholders in a way that promotes active communication is through virtual bulletin boards (e.g., Padlet). These interactive bulletin boards can be designed in many ways, all with a common aim to have constituents contribute to a collective conversation. This tool is a great way for individuals to share ideas through images, words, and sounds. Virtual bulletin boards provide an opportunity for an individual to share their perspective while also commenting on others. Furthermore, they enable individuals to organize ideas in a different format that may better align with how they express and process information.

Conclusion

Communication and collaboration are essential skills for leaders, driving both their success and the effectiveness of the departments they manage. Strong communication fosters trust, clarity, and alignment within teams and across departments, while collaboration enables resource sharing, innovation, and operational efficiency. Ultimately, a well-executed communication strategy and strong collaborative efforts can lead to improved student experiences, greater operational efficiency, and improved institutional outcomes. Considering the importance of effective communication and collaboration for higher education administrators, we lean on both the scholarship in this area as well as our professional experiences in offering a strategic guide to intentional communication and collaboration (see Appendix). We call on leaders to assess their current communication and collaboration practices, recognize areas for improvement, and adopt strategies that will enable them to lead more effectively.

References

Eddy, P. L. (2010). *Partnerships and collaborations in higher education: A critical examination of initiatives and practices.* Stylus.

Joshi, A., Zhang, K., Lasch, D., Beaudrie-Nunn, A., & Froerer, C. (2024). Mastering the art of managing up. *American Journal of Health-System Pharmacy, 81*(15), e398–e401. https://doi.org/10.1093/ajhp/zxae060

Morris, J. C., & Miller-Stevens, K. (2016). *Advancing collaboration theory: Models, typologies, and evidence.* Routledge. www.routledge.com/Advancing-Collaboration-Theory-Models-Typologies-and-Evidence/Morris-Miller-Stevens/p/book/9780815370369?srsltid=AfmBOopvRm7abJry_3529Muy0wNFhnEeCg4C3P_K5-WFRuE6SaLmacQ7

Northouse, P. (2016). *Leadership: Theory & practice* (7th ed.). Sage.

Appendix

Strategic Guide to Intentional Communication and Collaboration

Meeting Immediate and Short-Term Communication and Collaboration Needs

Identify primary internal stakeholders, create a regular communication plan, and establish areas for collaboration.

- Who is your direct supervisor?
    - How often will you have one-on-one meetings?
    - What kinds of communication expectations should be established (e.g., modes of communication preferences)?
    - What level of collaboration should be expected (e.g, creating or sustaining shared projects)?
- Who are you responsible for supervising?
    - How often will you have one-on-one meetings?
    - How often will you have team meetings?
    - What kinds of communication expectations should be established (e.g., modes of communication preferences)?
    - What level of collaboration should be expected (e.g, creating or sustaining shared projects)?
- Who are your counterparts (colleagues with similar position level)?
    - How often will you gather as a group?
    - What kinds of communication expectations should be established (e.g., modes of communication preferences)?
    - What level of collaboration should be expected (e.g, creating or sustaining shared projects)?

Establishing Strategic and Long-Term Communication and Collaboration Needs

- Identify secondary internal stakeholders, create a needs-based communication plan, and recognize potential areas for collaboration
    - Who are the members of your institution with whom you may not communicate regularly but impact or are impacted by your work (e.g., students, other offices, units, or divisions)?

- What channels of communication currently exist with these constituents (e.g., campus-wide emails)?
- What new channels of communication should be established (e.g., consistently distributed newsletters or community dialogues)?
- What are your long-term, strategic goals? How might secondary internal stakeholders serve as partners in achieving these goals? Are there areas for potential collaboration?
- What are your secondary internal stakeholders' needs? In what ways do these needs connect to your role and responsibilities? Are there areas for potential collaboration?

Identify external stakeholders, create a needs-based communication plan, and recognize potential areas for collaboration

- Who are your external stakeholders with whom you may not communicate regularly, but impact or are impacted by your work (e.g., alumni or community partners)?
  - What channels of communication currently exist with these constituents (e.g., campus-wide emails)?
  - What new channels of communication should be established (e.g., consistently distributed newsletters or community dialogues)?
  - What are your long-term, strategic goals? How might secondary internal stakeholders serve as partners in achieving these goals? Are there areas for potential collaboration?
  - What are your external stakeholders' needs? In what ways do these needs connect to your role and responsibilities? Are there areas for potential collaboration?

10

Everyone Recruits, Everyone Retains

Christian Alberto

For the past three years, you have served as the director of academic advising at a small, liberal arts college in Northern California. One day, you received an email from the institution's chief enrollment officer with the subject line: *New Initiative: Major Fair During Preview Day*.

Your heart sank as you skimmed the message. The college's leadership team decided it was important to incorporate a major fair into the annual preview day event for prospective students and their guests. The initiative was designed to provide attendees with a deeper understanding of academic programs – and despite your years of experience working in higher education – you were feeling overwhelmed. You were being asked to coordinate the college's representation at the fair. All of this included organizing academic departments, creating information booths for each major, and recruiting faculty and staff volunteers.

"Where does advising fit into that?" you muttered under your breath.

As someone who worked closely with students throughout their college journey, advising didn't seem to align with the numbers-driven world of enrollment. The idea of linking academic advising to bolstering enrollment seemed like an awkward fit. Still, with the leadership's directive, you knew you had no choice but to implement the program.

Over the following weeks, you began planning, trying to connect the dots. You met with department heads and faculty members, struggling to understand how a gathering of prospective students, who were still figuring out their interests, could translate into future enrollments.

On preview day, the major fair was set up in the student union. The tables were neatly arranged, each one representing a different major, from English to Engineering. Faculty members staffed booths, excited but still apprehensive about talking to prospective students and their families. You watched on anxiously, watching students wandering from booth to booth, asking questions and jotting down notes.

As the day wore on, you came to understand that the fair wasn't just about showing off departments. It was an early step in helping students visualize their future paths. It was about helping students to connect to both the academic and social offerings of the college. More importantly, it was about answering questions that would directly inform their decision to apply and enroll at the institution. It wasn't just about enrollment numbers – it was about helping students make informed decisions.

INTRODUCTION

As discussed in previous chapters, fiscal deficits have required increased enrollment and retention to generate revenue. Without a strong performance in these areas, an institution may fail to be sustainable over the long term. Therefore, it should be no surprise that leaders face increased pressure to ensure their institution's enrollment and retention rates remain robust.

To meet these challenges, enrollment managers have implemented enrollment management models and strategies to assist in achieving these goals. Everything higher education professionals do on campus, from interactions with students to the appearance of facilities and grounds, has the ability to impact recruitment and retention. Examples of a comprehensive approach (many of which are discussed below) include enhancing the academic and student experience, providing financial support, improving student services, and fostering a supportive campus culture. As changing demographics and competition among institutions continues to intensify, it becomes vital for institutions to differentiate themselves through a holistic approach to enrollment and retention. The following section explores how leaders can foster a recruitment- and retention-oriented mindset across their organization.

Enrollment Management

Within higher education, enrollment management can be defined as a strategic process used by institutions to attract and retain students while ensuring financial stability and success. It is a dynamic and multifaceted field that includes many stakeholders, policies, procedures and organizational structures that are designed in such a way to guide and support student enrollment and retention. Huddleston (2000), explains,

> Optimally, an institution's enrollment is comprehensively developed and is based on a strategic, integrative plan that includes the identification, attraction, selection, encouragement, registration, retention, and graduation of target student segments. The quality of the students' collegiate experience is based largely on the academic environment, operational excellence of the institution's transition programs, student services, and personal development opportunities. Within this broad context, an enrollment manager's efforts are intended to shape and influence particular units that have significant impact

on a student's decision to enroll, persist, and graduate. The strategic management of these units is important to an institution's growth, fiscal health, and student satisfaction.

(p. 65)

Prior to the 1970's admissions and retention processes, programs and services were less organized and structured. As a result of shifting demographics, less students enrolling, more institutions entering the marketplace, and higher institutional operating costs, leaders needed to guide institutions to intentionally support student enrollment and retention. Therefore, the concept of enrollment management as a profession was born. In the ever-changing educational environment, enrollment managers are often faced with the following obstacles that require careful consideration.

Defining Institutional Enrollment Goals

With the pressure to quantitatively achieve enrollment goals (make the class), there is additional campus attention to qualitatively achieve enrollment goals (shape the class). Making the class requires enrollment management to enroll enough students to meet bottom-line tuition revenue goals. Shaping the class requires additional evaluation on the academic preparedness of the class and additional goals may exist for balancing other demographic factors such as major, gender, race, ethnicity, geographic region, grade point average, and/or test scores, among others. This approach involves ensuring the campus is prepared to support the students it enrolls. Enrollment goals may focus on shaping the class with a lessened importance on student headcount.

Navigating Shifting Landscapes

Through the evolutions of higher education, enrollment managers are challenged to shape institutional responses to meet the ever-evolving and rapidly changing enrollment needs. To be successful, an enrollment management strategy must understand the broader context in which they operate and be prepared to pivot based on that understanding. As a comprehensive strategy, it involves integrating data-driven strategies throughout the entire student lifecycle, from recruitment to graduation.

With many options for students to choose from for higher education, enrollment managers guide institutions to answer the following questions:

- How can you ensure that despite the obstacles, institutions meet their enrollment and retention goals while staying true to their mission?
- How do students move throughout the enrollment funnel from prospective student to alumni?

Enrollment management strategies must not focus only on short-term goals, but on creating sustainable practices that will support institutional success for the long term. As a leader, it is important to act cohesively, think strategically, and be proactive in shaping a future where recruitment and retention efforts directly contribute to institutional growth, diversity, and academic excellence.

Aligning Institutional Resources

While defining institutional goals and adapting to shifting landscapes, enrollment managers are also coordinating an institutional response for enrollment sustainability. As students matriculate (enter) and graduate (exit) from institutions, there's a delicate balance in enrollment management to assist students to, and through, the degree programs. While graduating students is a key metric of success, enrollment managers must also ensure a steady pipeline of qualified candidates to sustain enrollment. One way this is achieved is by aligning institutional resources to support enrollment efforts. This alignment ensures that departments coordinate and align resources to strategically optimize enrollment. From marketing to financial aid, registrar, housing, student affairs and more, each department on campus has the ability to impact enrollment. A critical component of an effective enrollment strategy is how well institutions coordinate these campus efforts to support both recruitment and retention.

The Solution: Collaboration

Institutions that foster campus-wide collaboration have the potential to contribute to a strong enrollment management strategy. An example of an enrollment management collaboration is through the use of campus-wide committees to identify, and influence, policies for admissions and student retention that impact key milestones in the student experience. In this example, enrollment management becomes a centralized mechanism that evaluates the effectiveness of institutional practices and ensures alignment with overall institutional goals.

Drawing on the principles and strategies explored throughout this book, this chapter will examine best practices toward enrollment management collaboration to support students and institutional sustainability. From recruitment to retention, it is important for leaders to identify ways their unit can support enrollment goals for institutional sustainability. At the center of this exercise is answering how the unit supports students at the institution. The answer ultimately creates a mission statement for student centeredness. The following section's recommendations provide a lens for leaders to identify opportunities for impact. By implementing a student-centered approach that is responsive to both the changing landscape and the unique needs of applicants, leaders can successfully adapt to these challenges, ultimately positioning their institutions for long-term success.

Eight Best Practices Toward Enrollment Management Collaboration: Everyone Recruits, Everyone Retains

All individuals, regardless of their position or role within an institution, share the responsibility of supporting student recruitment and retention. This effort cannot be managed by a single individual with the words "recruitment" and "retention" in their title or confined to a specific department. From the vice president of enrollment management to the coordinator of campus experience, everyone plays an active role in both the student's decision to enroll and their continued success toward graduation. Promoting a recruitment and retention mindset requires a community-wide commitment, one that prioritizes a diverse student body and works to eliminate barriers to entry and success. The following sections explore how leaders across campus can foster a recruitment and retention-oriented mindset across their organization.

Know Your Student Body/Campus Demographics

Information is a key component to collaborative support in recruitment and retention. The more your unit is knowledgeable regarding the current state of the institution, from application numbers to admits to retention rates, the more individuals will feel compelled to assist. This understanding allows individuals to think beyond their day-to-day responsibilities to see the bigger picture. It also provides better insight into stakeholder views and opinions, also fostering a collaborative approach to problem solving and change. For example, knowing the average age of your incoming class or student body may change how an office chooses to engage with them (e.g., email versus text) and the types of programs being offered. Furthermore, there is a stronger likelihood of positive outcomes, thanks to access to more ideas and a broader awareness of the decisions being made by upper administrators.

Holistic Advising

Leaders should provide accessible advising and support services, helping students to navigate academic and career planning, while also addressing their personal development and overall well-being. For example, professional advisors should not only be aware of degree program requirements, but also have an awareness of student resources both on and off campus. For example, advisors should be aware of counseling and mental health–related services as well as peer-to-peer tutoring programs. At a minimum, departments can have brochures available for students or bulletin boards to share announcements and campus-wide updates.

Be Involved

Leaders (and departmental staff) should be involved in functions, initiatives, events, meetings, and programs on campus. When leaders are engaged, they contribute to an institutional culture that promotes student well-being and success. This makes prospective students more likely to enroll, but also helps students stay engaged and feel valued. It also helps to break down silos that exist between departments. This coordination allows for better allocation of resources and services (whether that be academic, social, or financial). This could involve attending student organization events or volunteering during residence hall move-in.

Student Participation

It is paramount to incorporate students in decision-making processes, which promote critical thinking and student participation. This allows functional areas to not only monitor student progress but make necessary adjustments in services and programming. Opportunities for student involvement could include serving as members of hiring committees, providing feedback on dining and other auxiliary services (e.g., dining or housing), or participating in a curriculum and policy review committee. Institutions that are able to effectively meet and exceed expectations will likely see higher rates of student satisfaction, retention, and success.

Share and Utilize Data

Data is crucial in student recruitment and retention, as it allows leaders to identify potential students, understand their unique needs and interests, proactively address potential challenges, and tailor outreach strategies to maximize the likelihood of enrollment, recruitment and, ultimately, graduation (Chapter 2). Potential sources of data could include, but are not limited to, application data, learning management software, student information systems, surveys, social media, and website engagement. Specific data points may include attendance, academic performance, demographic information, financial aid information, and employment and parental status to name a few. Some of these data points, such as attendance and academic performance, are clear indicators of student success. Others, such as distance from home, can be utilized in predictive analytics to identify at-risk students. By sharing information with colleagues regarding the student population at the institution, the likelihood of creating or sharing support services increases. For example, the basic needs center staff could obtain a report of economically disadvantaged students from the office of financial aid and direct them toward services offered at the center, such as financial, food, or housing support. Similarly, academic advisors could request a report of students with D, F, and W grades from the registrar each semester to collaborate with faculty and program leaders to develop cocurricular and wraparound support.

One way to encourage and foster dialogue has been to create a community of practice at your institution. Regular meetings of this group of leaders from across the university can analyze data from various sources, generate a work plan, and hold one another accountable. Overall, institutional data can empower leaders to make decisions that align with the institution's long-term strategic goals. Institutional research can significantly benefit an enrollment management strategy by providing data-driven insight into targeted recruitment strategies, enrollment trends, and financial aid strategies.

Task Force

Involvement in an institutional-wide committee, chaired by divisional leaders such as the vice provosts of enrollment, student affairs, and student success with representation from various campus departments (e.g., athletics, student involvement and leadership, marketing and communication, etc.) could serve as a useful forum for collaboration. Such a committee can assist in identifying factors that affect student enrollment and retention, four-year graduation/completion rates and improving the integration of the cocurricular and curricular endeavors. This approach encourages individuals to think beyond their often siloed functional areas and foster a deeper understanding of how their work contributes to the broader goals of enrollment management. Faculty members, in particular, can play a pivotal role on administrative committees such as this one, as they may have a deeper understanding of students' academic aptitude and leadership potential.

Review Policies and Procedures

Campus leaders can establish and promote an "everyone recruits and everyone retains" ethos by conducting regular comprehensive reviews of institutional and department policies and procedures. While used to define operations that impact student admission and engagement, this does not mean they are always equitable, fair, updated, or relevant. For example, this can involve reviewing admissions requirements and evaluation processes for fairness. One such instance is the decision to utilize standardized testing as a component of the evaluation process for applicants. Furthermore, college policies can significantly impact student retention by influencing factors like financial accessibility, academic support, flexibility in course schedules, and overall student well-being, ultimately determining whether students feel supported enough to stay enrolled and complete their degree. Examples may include policies related to need-based aid, academic standing (e.g., probation), and campus safety policies.

Engage Institutional Stakeholders

It is also essential to identify and collaborate with a broad spectrum of stakeholders from across the institution. It allows campus departments to leverage each other's strengths, create more comprehensive onboarding and enrollment experiences, develop strong systems to support students, identify potential challenges and obstacles early, and provide for a holistic experience that addresses the diverse needs of prospective and diverse students. The involvement of multiple stakeholders fosters a sense of shared responsibility for student success across the institution. As a leader in any functional area, it is imperative that you can identify key phases of the enrollment pipeline (e.g., how a student moves through the enrollment funnel) and significant milestones in the student experience. By identifying these markers and utilizing data, you can assess the effectiveness of policies, procedures, and programs and uncover areas where improvement is needed.

Faculty on Admissions Committees

Faculty on admissions committees play a pivotal role in shaping the diversity of incoming students, particularly regarding racial and ethnic representation. Their decisions, based on academic aptitude, leadership potential, and holistic assessments, significantly influence the composition of the student body. This underscores the importance of their role in promoting diversity in student admissions (NACAC, 2020).

Alumni and Professional Networks

Alumni and professionals are not just important but crucial in student recruitment, especially in specialized fields. Their influence, particularly those in the field, is significant, with most incoming graduate students citing professionals as key in their decision to pursue a specific field. This underscores the importance of strengthening ties between alumni relations and admissions to leverage alumni networks in recruitment and mentorship efforts. Additionally, alumni engagement significantly attracts students to specific programs (Chamberlain & Shuffelton, 2017).

Currently Enrolled and Prospective Students (Peer-to-Peer Recruitment)

Current students are vital in recruitment efforts, as their experiences can strongly influence prospective students. Engaging them in recruitment activities and promoting long-term support programs can reduce attrition and improve campus culture (Issenberg & Nason, 2018; Tinto, 2017). Peer-to-peer recruitment improves retention rates and fosters a more inclusive campus environment (Kalsbeek, 2013).

Undergraduate Advisors

Advisors are essential in guiding students toward career paths and graduate programs. Their collaboration with students is vital to ensure they are well-informed about admissions processes, institutional goals, and diversity initiatives, helping students make informed decisions (Pascarella & Terenzini, 2005; Sandeen, 2012). Advisors serve as trusted sources of information and significantly impact students' educational outcomes (Drake, 2011).

Financial Aid Counselors

Financial aid counselors are crucial in increasing access to higher education by providing information about scholarships, grants, and loans. Their collaboration with other campus departments is essential to ensure students have the financial support needed for retention and degree completion. Moreover, they can aid in financial literacy education, which has been identified as a key factor influencing student persistence and success (Dynarski & Scott-Clayton, 2013).

By recognizing the crucial roles of faculty, alumni, students, advisors, counselors, and financial aid teams, enrollment leaders can craft recruitment strategies that are inclusive, informed, and impactful. Collaboration among these stakeholders creates a more welcoming campus and fosters a shared responsibility for student success. A holistic approach to enrollment management is essential for driving effective, sustainable strategies that support student retention and academic excellence.

Conclusion

As the major fair unfolded on preview day, you found yourself watching students wander from booth to booth, questioning faculty and jotting down notes. What started as an overwhelming task, with a sense of disconnect between academic advising and enrollment, gradually became a clear objective. It wasn't just about showcasing majors – it was about helping prospective students visualize their future paths and empowering them to make informed decisions. In that moment, you realized how advising plays a critical role in enrollment, guiding students not just academically but through the decision-making process that ultimately shapes their college journey.

This chapter has emphasized that enrollment management is a collective effort. From understanding student demographics to aligning institutional resources, every department contributes to recruitment and retention. For a practical review on engaging your campus in this process, see the Appendix. By fostering a culture of collaboration, leaders can better support students and position their institutions for long-term success – ensuring each student's journey is shaped by possibility and purpose.

References

Chamberlain, M., & Shuffelton, A. (2017). The role of alumni networks in higher education. *Journal of Education Policy*, *32*(4), 412–425. https://doi.org/10.1080/02680939.2017.1283590

Dynarski, S., & Scott-Clayton, J. (2013). Financial aid policy: The role of counselors in higher education access. National Bureau of Economic Research. https://doi.org/10.3386/w19306

Huddleston, T., Jr. (2000). Enrollment management. *New Directions for Higher Education*, *2000*(111), 65–73.

Issenberg, S., & Nason, M. (2018). Peer-to-peer recruitment: A new approach to student recruitment. *Journal of Higher Education*, *89*(5), 712–734. https://doi.org/10.1080/00221546.2018.1435945

Kalsbeek, D. (2013). Student recruitment and retention: Peer to peer influence. *College and University Journal*, *88*(3), 24–35.

National Association for College Admission Counseling (NACAC). (2020). State of College Admission. www.nacacnet.org/state-of-college-admission-report/

Pascarella, E. T., & Terenzini, P. T. (2005). *How college affects students: A third decade of research* (Vol. 2). Jossey-Bass.

Sandeen, C. (2012). The role of advising in the student experience. *Journal of College Student Development*, *53*(6), 825–828. https://doi.org/10.1353/csd.2012.0086

Tinto, V. (2017). *Dropping out of college: The causes and consequences of student attrition* (2nd ed.). University of Chicago Press.

Appendix

Enrollment Management as a Collective Effort

Much like the eight best practices above, it's important for you to find yourself in the practical application to determine how your unit contributes to the success of enrollment at your institution. In the introduction of this chapter, an open house/preview day was highlighted to outline how easily an academic advising office contributes to enrollment. Expanding on this thought, the practical application will demonstrate ways an enrollment management office engages everyone on campus in the planning stages of an open house.

The purpose of an open house is to present the campus culture, values, and student experience to individuals involved in the college decision making-process. Students are visiting campus, with influential decision-makers (e.g., guardians, parents, neighbors, school counselors, friends). With many options to choose from, institutions use preview days to share their campus with prospective students. Enrollment managers who plan a successful open house involve the entire campus.

Campus Department	Potential Collaboration
Business Services	Budget and Procurement Planning
Campus Events	Room and Building Reservations
Registrar	Classroom Reservations for Breakout Sessions
University Web	RSVP
Marketing	Invitations, Campus News Announcement, Step and Repeat, Campus Maps
Printing Services	Agenda, Signage for Directions and Sessions
Parking Services	Guest Parking (Reservations, Validation)
Campus Police	Additional Security, Road Blocks
Facilities	Tables and Chairs, Stage, Podium, etc.
Ground Services	Pre-Cleaning, Additional trash cans, landscaping in advance
Dining Services	Breakfast Items, Lunch, Snack or Coffee Stations/Capacity at Dining Halls
Information Technology	Presentation Laptops and Projectors/Guest Wi-Fi Access
Residence Life/Housing	Tour Room Coordination

(continued)

Campus Department	Potential Collaboration
Campus Bookstore	Premium Giveaways/Extended Hours/ Coupons/Preparation for Additional Traffic
Athletics	Mascot and/or Cheerleaders, Breakout Session, Campus Resource Fair
President and Provost Office	Welcome Speech or Video
Student Government Association/Homecoming Court	Welcome Speech or Video
Marching Band	Opening Welcome
Alumni Office	Alumni Panel, Campus Resource Fair
Admissions	Campus Tours, Application Workshops
Financial Aid	Breakout Sessions/Campus Resource Fair
Academic Departments/ Programs/Colleges (Faculty)	Breakout Sessions/Campus Resource Fair
International Services	Breakout Sessions/Campus Resource Fair
Career Services	Breakout Sessions/Campus Resource Fair
Honors	Breakout Sessions/Campus Resource Fair
Undergraduate Research	Breakout Sessions/Campus Resource Fair
Recreation & Wellness Center	Tour and Campus Resource Fair
Health Services	Campus Resource Fair
Counseling Services	Campus Resource Fair
Student Activities	Breakout Session/Campus Resource Fair
Greek Life	Campus Resource Fair
Student Organizations	Campus Resource Fair
Graduate School	Campus Resource Fair
ROTC	Campus Resource Fair
Tutoring Services/ Supplemental Instruction	Campus Resource Fair
Pre-Professional Programs	Breakout Session/Campus Resource Fair
Cashier & Student Accounts	Campus Resource Fair

11

Conclusion

Carlos Gooden and Mike Hoffshire

Conclusion

As institutions continue to adapt and respond to external environmental factors, it is inevitable that managers must be proactively prepared to navigate and lead through changes. Successfully navigating these changes requires more than ambition to succeed; rather, leaders must have a formalized plan to create a strong operational infrastructure. Achieving greater operational efficiency requires structure, intentionality, and a deep understanding of the common operational components of success. As a result, this book was developed to fill a critical gap in higher education leadership by offering a practical framework and tools for building and sustaining efficient units/offices. Grounded in the lived experiences of practitioners, the ten infrastructure components outline tools that leaders need to assess, enhance, and strengthen their unit's operations.

To support a comprehensive reflection, Table 11.1 reviews the components and includes the content covered in this text.

As a reminder, the practical applications empower readers to begin making an immediate impact in their workspaces.

TABLE 11.1 Infrastructural Component Descriptions and Practical Applications

Infrastructural Component	Brief Description	Practical Application
Navigating Context & Change	Outlined tools for assessing institutional values and influential factors that inform campus norms.	Navigating context and campus culture within the ten infrastructure components
Data	Described the importance and uses of quantitative and qualitative data.	Sample queries a manger may collect
Budget	Focused on understanding budgets, revenues and expenses.	Sample appropriations for a departmental budget
Strategic Planning	Provided structure to develop a strategic plan.	Sample table of contents for a departmental strategic plan
University Policies & Procedures	Reviewed the importance of understanding federal/state laws and institutional policies that guide a leader's work.	Key policy and procedures
Day-to-Day Operations	Discussed the importance (and how to) of developing a daily operations manual.	Sample table of contents for a policy and procedure manual
Organizational Chart & Staffing	Reviewed common organizational types, roles and responsibilities, and insight in how to manage staff turnover.	Steps to create an organizational chart
Training & Development	Provided strategies for successful onboarding, training, professional development and performance management of staff.	Sample onboarding agenda; performance management outline
Communication & Collaboration	Examined the critical role of communication and collaboration.	Strategic guide to intentional communication and collaboration
Enrollment Management	Provided a detailed overview of enrollment management.	Enrollment management as a collective effort

Although this text orders the infrastructure components sequentially, managers are encouraged to examine their context to determine their starting point. Think about previous roles and positions within organizations you may have held. To assist in this reflective process, we pose the following five questions:

1. What components did your previous manager(s) do really well?
2. What components did your previous manager(s) have room to grow in?
3. Over the past 12 months, what components of office management have consumed a majority of your time?
4. When thinking about managing an office/division, what structural components would you like to develop?
5. What are the current needs and expectations of your role (by your team, supervisor, institution)?

With the answers to these questions, you are taking the first step in applying the infrastructure components in the workplace. As leaders embrace these components, the editors highlight five key acknowledgements for consideration when applying the model. Depending on your responses, you may discover new themes (or priorities) that are not reflected in the ten infrastructure components, but require immediate attention. The discovery of new themes is not only expected, but encouraged. More importantly, you may identify a different starting point than "Navigating Context and Change" as the infrastructure component to start (and that is also okay).

Acknowledgment 1: Components Are Not Linear

Although the components were presented sequentially, this model is not linear. The editors engaged in many conversations surrounding the placement of the infrastructural components, ultimately avoiding a ranked or numbered approach. Much of your starting point will depend on the current priorities of your institution and timing in the academic calendar. We understand that where one organization is in their cycle or development may be different from another. While one leader may choose to engage with their budget to meet an institutional deadline, another may choose to begin with training and development to immediately on-board new staff. As an adaptive model, there is no right or wrong starting point.

Acknowledgment 2: Components Are Not Exhaustive

As editors, we selected the ten components that we believe are the most important in creating an efficient, student-centered functional unit. However, arguments could be made to swap out or replace our components with others. It is important we acknowledge that the core infrastructure components are not exhaustive. For example, consideration can also be extended to relevant themes of learning and leveraging technology (e.g., CRM, SIS, or early alert systems) or navigating campus emergencies. Other relevant considerations can be made for professional development, safety and risk management, or navigating workplace conflict as potential component additions. The incorporation of components largely depends on the situational needs of the institution, the expectations of your supervisor, and current demands of the role.

Acknowledgment 3: Efficiency Takes Time

Each of the ten infrastructure components includes multistep processes that require time and focus. Achieving greater operational efficiency can be daunting to navigate while also managing routine manager duties such as attending meetings, juggling projects, and balancing day-to-day responsibilities. Indeed, it is not practical to expect readers to learn, address, and complete each component in a week, month, or semester/term. Rather, incremental progress across components is expected. One week, you might draft a table of contents for an operational manual; while in the same stretch of time, you could also schedule a half-day retreat for strategic planning. Meanwhile, progress on other components – such as data or budgeting – may stall temporarily, and that's perfectly fine. It's important to not get overwhelmed by all of the advice and recommendations in this text, but instead, use this as a reference guide to make progress over time.

Acknowledgment 4: Diversity, Equity, Inclusion, and Belonging

Foundational to this text is how diversity, equity, inclusion, and belonging (DEIB) are a critical part of the leadership process; however, readers will notice that DEIB is not a separate and standalone infrastructure component. This was intentional on behalf of the editors, believing that leaders should strive to incorporate and embed DEIB-related conversations, education, and implementation into all ten infrastructural components. Integrating DEIB into all leadership actions is crucial for creating a more inclusive workplace, fostering innovation, and improving organizational performance. Leaders who prioritize DEIB actively shape a culture where everyone feels included, which leads to better employee engagement and ultimately, student success. The following are examples of how leaders can incorporate a DEIB lens into each of the infrastructural components:

- Data: When requesting data for trend analysis or metric monitoring, it is best practice to disaggregate the data by groups or cohorts to better understand the unique patterns by group. This helps to better understand trends by population to further inform strategy. Utilizing a DEIB lens, this may involve disaggregating data points by race, age, gender, region, or even socioeconomic status to truly be effective in achieving student-centeredness.
- Day-to-Day Operations: Cultural awareness is critical in the development of office policies and procedures manual. Recognizing that a staff member may need time off for cultural or religious reasons, like Indigenous Peoples Day, Yom Kippur, or Ramadan. A PPM leave policy with blackout days that do not consider these factors can create tension and conflict with our values. By anticipating potential conflicts, you, as a leader, can proactively plan and foster belonging in the workplace.
- Training and Development: A DEIB framework would center onboarding materials and staff integration (e.g., team building) around the needs of the staff (both individually and collectively). DEIB materials that explicitly address DEIB

principles can help new hires understand the organization's commitment to inclusivity. Also, developing team-building activities that offer options where people can engage in different ways or levels also promotes such a culture.

By integrating DEIB into each infrastructural component, leaders are better positioned to create organizations where colleagues, direct reports, and stakeholders are valued and supported through intentional actions. As leaders, we have a responsibility to be mindful of workplace conditions and the cultures we either create, curate, or promulgate. It is important to remember that the decisions you make will have implications for others, which then has the potential to impact those on our team. More than just an acknowledgement, the editors assert that leaders should hold space to think critically about power dynamics and systemic barriers. Additionally, it is important to acknowledge the impact of the environmental conditions that we as leaders create for others. From this standpoint, the integration of DEIB into each infrastructural component is not a footnote or minor recommendation; rather, it is essential to achieving the goals of the unit and achieving operational efficiency.

Acknowledgment 5: One Resource Among Many

This book is intended to be a starting point toward achieving operational efficiency; however, it is not the sole resource that should be used when looking to position the unit for success. This book provides tangible resources that, when paired with additional professional development opportunities, becomes part of a larger strategy for managers in higher education. The editors advise managers to lean into their local, state, and national governing associations, seek out podcasts, blogs, or consult with mentors that can strengthen areas of management and leadership.

Putting It All Together: Maya's Implementation of the Components

The final section of this chapter illustrates a case study to operationalize the infrastructural components in action. The example below provides a practical look at how these components can be applied in real-world leadership scenarios.

Maya has been employed at her organization for seven years. In her role as a senior director, she led a team of ten professional staff members and five interns. Nine months ago, following her supervisor's departure, Maya was appointed interim assistant vice president (AVP) for the division of student affairs. In this expanded role, she now oversees 5 functional areas, managing a team of 35 professionals and twelve interns.

Just 30 days into her new role, Maya learned that her division would inherit another functional unit, international programs and services due to a university organizational restructure. This change coincided with an upcoming deadline to submit division-wide strategic plans to the president.

Although Maya is a seasoned professional, this level of leadership is new to her. Maya must now develop an operational infrastructure and strategic plan to support the division, her staff, and the students they serve. In response to these evolving demands, Maya quickly develops an updated organizational chart to clarify reporting lines, roles, and responsibilities. She also distributes a policy and procedure manual to assist with day-to-day operations. To strengthen communication and collaboration within the team, she created an outlook calendar to detail key dates and events across the division and also launched a Zoom chat to support prompt communication responses to questions and to facilitate stronger engagement for employees who are working remotely. With these foundational systems in place, Maya turns her attention to training and development, which includes cross-training staff on key protocols and workflows. At the same time, Maya must learn the university's budgeting process, understand laws and policies that affect units in their division, and meet with relevant stakeholders across the institution to understand the working relationships of her department, collaboration opportunities, and current priorities. She also begins collecting data to inform the foundation of the divisional strategic plan.

Maya's case illustrates the ways in which the flexible implementation of the infrastructural components can be critical to successful leadership. She did not engage with all ten components at once, nor were they addressed in the sequential order presented in this text. You'll notice that no attention was given to the infrastructural components of navigating context and change and enrollment management. Her leadership decisions toward operational efficiency were driven by the immediate needs of her role and the institutional context. Scenarios like Maya's can be all too common when it comes to the ever-changing, and unpredictable, landscape in higher education. Leadership is rarely straightforward – it requires adaptability, foresight, and responsiveness to shifting conditions. Maya's journey underscores that the ten infrastructure components are not a checklist to complete, but a cycle of ongoing, intentional organizational work. Her example highlights that operational efficiency is a continuous process, rooted in leadership.

Closing Thoughts

This book serves as both a playbook and a guide for new, mid-level, and senior leaders in higher education. This text is intended to provoke reflection, encourage proactive planning, and empower leaders to take ownership of their departments. More importantly, the practical applications serve as a resource that can be used daily. As explored in each chapter, navigating toward operational efficiency is not a one-time initiative but an ongoing commitment to strategic, intentional, and thoughtful management. Whether navigating budgeting, staff turnover, or responding to institutional changes, the chapters have addressed key elements of effective operational leadership. Each of these elements plays a vital role in maintaining smooth administrative operations and ensuring that both staff and students receive the support they need to succeed. It is important to note these components were created in the spirit of preparing leaders for success in higher education. When leaders focus on building a strong infrastructure, there are several winners in this process – the campus colleagues, the staff, the institution, and the students.

Index

academic catalog 58, 64; undergraduate policies, and 59
accountability: conversations 70; data 13, 24; informality 87; professional development 97–100; strategic planning 47
actual budget 31–2
additional resources advocacy 38
ADKAR® Model 8–9
admissions office: external constituents 107; intelligence cycle, and 22–4
advising 118–19; holistic 124–5
alumni 128
Americans with Disabilities Act (ADA) 55, 63
audits: organizational structure 89; policies 54
awareness: change, and 8; self 2–3, 10

Bolman, L. 6–7
budgeting models 32–5; data-based decision-making, and 38–9; practical tools 36–8
budgets 28–31; balancing act 27–8; process 31–2; shortfalls 27, 31, 119; statewide policies, and 56–7; strategic plan costs 47–8; training and development 95
business intelligence cycle 16–22

Cal Grant 56
centralized approaches 32–4
change: definition 5–6; drivers of readiness 6; strategic planning, and 41; ten infrastructural components, within 10–12
collaboration: benefits 109–10; communication, and 104; data 22; definition 105–6; enrollment management, and 123, 131–2; importance 109–11; strategic guide 116–17; tools 111–14
communication: collaboration, and 104; definition 105; expectations 76–7, 116; importance 107–9; senior administrators 109; strategic guide 116–17; teams, among 108–9; tools 111–14
context: campus culture 4–5; ten infrastructural components, within 10–12
cross-training 96
cultural change perspective 8
culture: elements 4–5; internal policy, and 73–4; questions 5

data: analysis 20–1, 24; collection 18–19, 23; diversity, equity, inclusion, and belonging (DEIB) 137; framework 16–22; infrastructure components, macro-level 15–16; micro-level 14–15; purposes 14–16; share and utilize 125–6; steps to take 17; tool, as 13
day-to-day operations: balancing philosophies and operations 75–6; benefits of a manual 68–73; case studies 66–8, 75; contextualize university policy 68; cross-training and turnover 66; customer service standards 67; diversity, equity, inclusion, and belonging (DEIB) 137; institutional policies, and 65; safety and risk management 67–8
Deal, T. 6–7
decentralized approaches 32, 35

Index

decision-making: culture 4–5; data, and 14, 24–5; self-awareness 2; strategic planning, and 36
departmental policy and procedure manual (PPM): benefits 68–70; contents 71, 77–9; developing 70–3; need for 62, 65; purpose 65–6; reflection of values, as 73–6
dissemination 21–2; communication, and 104; departmental policy and procedure manual (PPM) 72; example 24
diversity, equity, inclusion, and belonging (DEIB) 76; integration 137–8
documentation 48

Employee Handbook 59–60, 64
enrollment management 120–3; best practice 123–9; collaboration, and 123, 131–2; data, and 15–16; defining goals 121; definition 120; resources alignment 122–3; shifting landscapes 121–2
equal employment opportunity (EEO) policies 59–60
events planning 58, 64
evolutionary change perspective 8
expenses 29–31, 40
external stakeholders 107, 117
external training 96

faculty on admissions committees 128
Family and Medical Leave Act (FMLA) 60
Family Educational Rights and Privacy Act (FERPA) 55, 63
federal policies 54–6; higher education, in 55
feedback loops 72
financial aid counselors 129
financial reporting 28–9
flat structure 83–4
focus groups 111–12
formula-based budgeting 34
four framework Approach 6–7
free tuition programs 57
functional structure 84–5
funding guidance 28, 30

goal creation 46–7
grievance procedures 60
guiding philosophies 74

hierarchal structure 81–82
Higher Education Act (HEA) 55, 63; funding 56
horizontal reporting lines 84–5
human resource frame 7
hybrid budgeting approaches 35

incremental budgeting 33–4
infographics 112
information: campus demographics 124; processing 19–20, 23; storage 20, 23
institutional change perspective 8
institutional policies 58–9; day-to-day operations, and 62–3; developing operations manual 71; practical application 61–2
internal stakeholders 106–7, 116
internal training 95–6

Jeanne Clery Disclosure of Campus Security Policy and Campus Crime Statistics Act (Clery Act) 55, 63
job descriptions: creation 86; reviewing 87

key milestones 44
key performance metrics 18
Kezar, A. 7–8

lunch and learn 112

macro-level policies 54
matrix structure 85
measurements 47
messaging platforms 112–13
mission, institutional: budgets, and 27, 30, 35; data 17–18; job

roles, and 87; progress 15, 113; strategic planning 43–4, 49; student centredness 123; understanding 5
monitoring and evaluation: budget 37; continuous improvement 73; performance (*see* performance evaluation); strategic planning 48–9
multiple change perspective approach 7–8

National Association of College and University Business Officers (NACUBO) guidance 28, 30; using 37

onboarding 61–2, 93–4; sample agenda 101–2
one-on-one meetings 113
order of infrastructure components 2
organizational chart (org chart) 80–1, 89; creating 90–1; types 81–5
organizational structures 82

partnerships: benefits 104–5; requirements 110
peer-to-peer recruitment 128
performance evaluations 58, 64, 99; need for 98
performance improvement plan (PIP) 99–100
performance management: inclusive 97–8; outline 102–3; process 98
Performance Partnership Pilot ("P3") for Disconnected Youth 55–6
personal inventory assessment 3
planning to plan 44
policy changes 54–5
policy review 127
political change perspective 8
political frame 7
post-hire 93–4
preview day 118–19, 129–30
probationary period review 98–9
professional development 94–7; addressing 95–7; assessing 94–5

professional networks 128
professional resources 97
projected budget 31–2
promotions 87–8
purchasing policy 60–1

qualitative data 18
quantitative data 18

recruitment 119, 123–4; and retention-oriented mindset 124–9
regulatory compliance 53–4
reports 113
responsibility center management (RCM) 35
retention 119, 123–4; and recruitment-oriented mindset 124–9
revenue 29; generation 119
risk management 58, 64
roles and responsibilities 86–8; clarity, ensuring 86–7
rules of engagement 1–2

salary expenditure 30
scenario planning 71
scientific management perspective 7
self-awareness 2–3; importance 10
shared responsibility 110
shared vision 41, 44, 50
social cognition change perspective 8
speaking as budget expert 37
staff leave 60; case study 75
staff turnover 88–9; documenting processes 88–9; transition planning 89
stakeholders: data sharing 21; identification 106–7; institutional engagement 127–9; strategic planning 45
state education budget allocations (public institutions) 57, 63
state financial aid policies 57, 63
statewide policies 56–7
statewide workforce development policies 57

storytelling 21–2, 24–5, 36
strategic planning: adaptability, and 41–2; benefits 49; budgeting, and 36; challenges 49–50; components 43; example contents 51–2; failures to use 42; guiding principles 43–9; importance 41; literature 42–3; priorities 36
structural frame 7
student participation 125
surveys 113–14
symbolic frame 7

task definition 17–18, 23
task force 126–7
team engagement 44–5; communication among 108; developing operations manual 72
team time protection 96
ten infrastructural components 134; case study 138–40; context and change, within 10–12; diversity, equity, inclusion, and belonging (DEIB) 137; non-exhaustive 136; not linear 135–6; one resource of many 138; reflection 135; time needed 136
360-degree review 99

Title IX 55, 63
town halls 114
tracking strategic plan 47
training 94–7; addressing 95–7; assessing 94–5; diversity, equity, inclusion, and belonging (DEIB) 137–8
transparency 75
travel policy 60–1, 64
TRIO programs 53–4
tuition regulation policies 57

undergraduate advisors 129

values: budgets, and 32; collaboration, and 72; influence 8; new team members 93; performance management 98, 100; self-awareness, and 2–3; strategic planning 49
values-driven policy 73–6
vertical reporting lines 81, 84–5
video conferencing platforms 114
visual tools 22

work-life harmony 76

zero-based budgeting 32–3

For Product Safety Concerns and Information please contact our EU representative GPSR@taylorandfrancis.com
Taylor & Francis Verlag GmbH, Kaufingerstraße 24, 80331 München, Germany

www.ingramcontent.com/pod-product-compliance
Lightning Source LLC
Chambersburg PA
CBHW061717300426
44115CB00014B/2723